1,411 QI FACTS

John Lloyd is the founder of QI. He was the original producer of *The News Quiz*, *To the Manor Born*, *Not the Nine O'Clock News*, *Spitting Image* and *Blackadder*. He is now the presenter of QI's sister show, BBC Radio 4's *The Museum of Curiosity*. His favourite page is 322.

John Mitchinson was QI's very first researcher. Before that, he published authors as diverse as Haruki Murakami, The Beatles and a woman who knitted with dog hair. He is now the co-founder of Unbound, the innovative crowd-funding publisher. His favourite page is 204.

James Harkin, QI's Head Elf, is known as 'Turbo' for his phenomenal work rate. A former mathematician, physicist and pub accountant, he now co-presents the QI Elves' podcast *No Such Thing As A Fish* and co-produces *The Museum of Curiosity*. His favourite page is 319.

A QUITE INTERESTING BOOK

1,411 QI FACTS

TO KNOCK YOU SIDEWAYS

Compiled by
John Lloyd, John Mitchinson
& James Harkin

with the QI Elves
Anne Miller, Andrew Hunter Murray,
Anna Ptaszynski & Alex Bell

ff

FABER & FABER

First published in 2014
by Faber & Faber Ltd
Bloomsbury House
74–77 Great Russell Street
London WC1B 3DA
This paperback edition first published in 2016

Typeset by Ian Bahrami
Printed in England by CPI Group (UK) Ltd,
Croydon CR0 4YY

All cover images courtesy of Shutterstock unless otherwise
stated: Flamingo © David Dea, Boxing Glove © Ljupco
Smokovski, Pipework © rodho / donatas1205 / EsHanPhot /
Africa Studio, Ladybirds © Kletr, Spacewalk © 3Dsculptor /
Fer Gregory, Evolution © Nicolas Primola, ASL fingerspelling
© VILevi. Japanese script of Showa Emperor - Public Domain.
BASL fingerspelling © Kathy Dewar / Getty. Einstein ©
Ullstein Bild / Getty. Mammoth © Nicolas Primola / iStock

A CIP record for this book
is available from the British Library

ISBN 978–0–571–32984–7

FSC
www.fsc.org
MIX
Paper from
responsible sources
FSC® C101712

2 4 6 8 10 9 7 5 3 1

Contents

[v]

Introduction

*Now, what I want is, Facts. Teach these
boys and girls nothing but Facts. Facts
alone are wanted in life.*
CHARLES DICKENS, *Hard Times* (1854)

We've taken the opening lines of Dickens's shortest novel to heart. Here are facts, facts, facts, 1,411 times over.

If you don't believe any of them, or want to explore the background detail, go to our website, qi.com/1411, and type the page number into the search box. Because, much as we love them, we know that facts don't tell the whole story.

They also don't last. Unlike buildings, facts aren't set in stone. Like milk or meat, they have a sell-by date.

In 2013, a Harvard mathematician called Samuel Arbesman wrote a book called *The Half-Life of Facts*, in which he compares facts to uranium atoms. Individually, their lifespan is unpredictable, but lumped together we can accurately predict that half the atoms will decay within 4.47 billion years — the so-called 'half-life' of uranium 238. Facts, it turns out, also have a half-life, and most of them don't last nearly as long.

For example, it's only a few hundred years since everybody agreed that the Sun went round the Earth. Only half a century ago, doctors thought smoking was good for you. Only eight years ago, it was a 'fact' that Pluto was a planet, until it was downgraded by the International Astronomical Union in 2006.

Arbesman is an expert in scientometrics — the science of science — and he has shown that the time it takes to overturn half of any given body of knowledge can be measured. The subject with the longest half-life is mathematics, much of which, alone among human knowledge, appears to be immortal. Alarmingly, one of the shortest-lived disciplines is medicine – where it can be shown that half of what doctors believe to be true will be proven wrong within 45 years. The problem is, of course, they don't know *which* half.

Information is fleeting. Human records are broken; new particles are discovered; fresh historical documents come to light. Dinosaurs turn out not to be giant grey iguanas after all, but multicoloured feathery proto-birds of all shapes and sizes. Right now, even the daddy of all facts, the Big Bang theory, is looking wobbly.

Almost all that is now obvious will one

day be seen as ludicrous. So what you hold in your hands isn't really a fact book at all; it's a situation report on what we think we know at this particular moment in time.

And that's fine with us. We like facts not so we can boast about them, but because they make us think. Because they challenge our preconceptions, not reinforce them.

So we hope you enjoy reading these facts as much as we've enjoyed finding them. But don't dawdle – you don't know how long they have left to live.

JOHN LLOYD, JOHN MITCHINSON
& JAMES HARKIN

*Those who love wisdom must
investigate many things.*
HERACLITUS (*c.*535–*c.*475 BC)

@

There are 1,411 tigers
left in India.

The Greek
for 'left-handed'
also means 'better'.

The 'Heil Hitler' salute
is legal in Switzerland
as long as it's an expression
of personal opinion.

Qatar is the only country
that begins with a Q and
Iraq is the only country
that ends with one.

The letter Q
was illegal in Turkey
for 85 years.

Dildos
are illegal in Texas.

Snake charming
is illegal in India.

In New Zealand,
snakes of any kind
are illegal.

In the Second World War,
the Allies had a plan to drop
boxes of poisonous snakes
on enemy troops.

On D-Day,
J. D. Salinger fought
with six chapters of
The Catcher in the Rye
in his backpack.

Charles Darwin let his children
use the original manuscript
of *On the Origin of Species*
as drawing paper.

Charles Dickens's family had
a cat, seven dogs, two ravens,
a canary called Dick and
a pony called Newman Noggs.

Theodore Roosevelt
had guinea pigs called
Admiral Dewey, Bishop Doane,
Dr Johnson, Father O'Grady and
Fighting Bob Evans,
and a small bear
called Jonathan Edwards.

Anton Chekhov
had a pet mongoose.

In 1849,
the Viceroy of Egypt
gave London Zoo a hippo
in exchange for a greyhound.

There are more
plastic flamingos
in the US than
real flamingos.

(Q)

There are more
statues of lions in the world
than there are real lions.

Two-thirds
of the world's polar bears
live in Canada.

When Canada
held a competition
to design its national flag,
more than 10% of the entries
featured a beaver.

The biggest dam
built by beavers
is twice as long
as the Hoover Dam.

There is enough concrete
in the Hoover Dam
to build a road across the US
from coast to coast.

The first motor insurance policy
issued by Lloyd's of London
described the car as a
'ship navigating on land'.

The first fatal car accident
in the UK was caused by
a driver going at
4 mph.

6%
of drivers
deliberately swerve
to kill animals.

You are 20 times more likely to
die in an accident at home
than you are to win the
National Lottery.

In 2007,
210,000 Americans
were injured by lawnmowers.

The lawnmower is
the most dangerous item
in the garden.
The second most dangerous
is the flowerpot.

When Edwin Beard Budding
invented the lawnmower,
he tested it at night
so no one would think
he was mad.

Using a petrol-driven lawnmower
for one hour produces
as much air pollution
as a 100-mile car trip.

It is illegal in Chicago
for lawns to have weeds
more than 10 inches tall.

Plants suffer from
sexually transmitted diseases.

Orchids can get
jet lag.

In Mogadishu,
the capital of Somalia,
there is only one flower shop.

There is only one stop sign
in the whole of Paris.

The name sign of
the town of Lost
in Aberdeenshire
is the only one in Britain
that is welded to its pole.

Female strawberry poison frogs
have only one way of choosing
a male to mate with:
which one is closest.

A male capuchin monkey
will have sex with any female
that throws a stone at him.

In 2003,
Morocco offered Iraq
2,000 monkeys
to help them
detonate mines.

The Burmese sneezing monkey
sneezes uncontrollably
whenever it rains.

5% of cats
are allergic to humans.

Napoleon, Mussolini and Hitler
were all scared of cats.

If cats don't encounter people
by the time they're 10 weeks old,
they will always be scared of them.

Human beings
have as many brain cells
in their stomachs
as cats have in their brains.

A cat's brain can store
1,000 times more data
than an iPad.

The human brain has
the same percentage of fat
as clotted cream.

Camel urine
is as thick as syrup.

Whale milk
has the consistency
of toothpaste.

Toothpaste
is addictive for bears
but toxic to dogs.

New-car smell
is toxic to humans.

The human nose
can recognise over
1,000,000,000,000
different smells.

You can tell
if a duck has bird flu
by smelling its droppings.

The smell of a man
is as stressful to mice
as a three-minute swim.
The smell of women
doesn't bother them.

Women
have been awarded
only four of the
406 George Crosses.

Until the First World War,
offices for women had
separate entrances and staircases,
for reasons of 'morality'.

Women
weren't allowed to serve
on Royal Navy submarines
until 2011.

Girls in the UK
have been getting
higher grades than boys
at school and university
for nearly a century.

Female students in China
outperform men
to such an extent that
some universities have
introduced a male quota.

There are enough
empty homes in China
for everyone in the UK
to have one each.

If they were countries,
the Chinese provinces of
Guangdong, Shandong,
Henan, Sichuan and Jiangsu
would be among the
world's 20 most populous.

China gets a new skyscraper
every five days.

China is
the world's largest consumer
of red wine.

More wine is drunk per head
in Vatican City
than any other country on Earth.

The crew of the *Marie Celeste*
left 1,700 barrels of alcohol
behind them.

Between 1908 and 1965,
Winston Churchill drank
42,000 bottles of champagne.

By the time
a glass of champagne goes flat,
two million bubbles
will have popped.

In Beijing,
two million people
live underground.

In 1870,
two million rabbits
were killed every year in Australia,
all descended from just 24
released in 1859.

The soil in
your back garden is
two million years old.

Oxford University
was over 300 years old
when the Aztec Empire
was founded.

When Harvard University
was founded,
Galileo was still alive.

Charles Darwin
and Abraham Lincoln were
born on the same day
in 1809.

In 1941,
there were only
11 democracies
in the world.

When the Pyramids were built
woolly mammoths still
roamed the Earth.

Sir Bruce Forsyth
is four months older
than sliced bread.

The *Radio Times*
is 12 days older
than Nicholas Parsons.

Nobody knows
how old the
Grand Canyon is.

From 1974 to 1976,
Shirley Temple was
US Ambassador to Ghana.

Shirley Temple
always had exactly
56 curls in her hair.

An *acersecomic*
is a person who
has never had a haircut.

Wealthy ancient Egyptians
slept with neck supports
rather than pillows
to preserve their hairstyles.

The average person in Coventry
sleeps for 6 hours
and 5 minutes
a night.

Two-thirds of parents
who sing their children to sleep
prefer pop music
to lullabies.

People in Britain
who wake in the middle of the night
are most likely to do it
at 3.44 a.m.

One o'clock in the morning
is the peak time
for moth activity.

There are 2,500 species
of moth in the UK
but only 60 species
of butterfly.

The greater wax moth
can hear sounds that are
more high-pitched than
any known animal
can make.

Humans
speak more languages
than there are species of mammal.

The more rivers an area has,
the more languages will
evolve there.

Esperanto is the only language
with no irregular verbs.

Black Americans and white Americans
have different versions of
American Sign Language.

The sign for the female sex (♀)
represents the hand mirror
of the Roman goddess Venus.

The inventor of roller skates
first demonstrated them
by hurtling into a party
while playing the violin
and crashing into a huge mirror.

Police cars
in Dubai
can go at
267 mph.

A cheetah
that sprints for
more than 30 seconds
can suffer brain damage.

Ladybirds
can fly
as fast as racehorses
can run.

When threatened,
a limpet can run away
at a speed of
two inches an hour.

The Chilean word *achaplinarse*
means to run about in
the style of Charlie Chaplin.

The Chilean word
for plumber
is *gasfiter*.

Gavisti,
the Sanskrit word for 'war',
literally translates as
'desire for more cows'.

Greece is
the only country in the world
whose name contains
none of the letters
in the word 'Olympiads'.

George Eyser,
who won three golds,
two silvers and a bronze
at the 1904 Olympics,
had a wooden leg.

Olympic medal-winners
live almost three years
longer than the rest of us.

Sports journalists were banned
from the first modern Olympics
as they were considered to be
professional sportspeople.

Michael Phelps
has won more Olympic golds
than India, Nigeria, North Korea,
Portugal, Taiwan and Thailand
combined.

Ⓠ

Olympic swimmers
routinely pee in the pool.

In wine-tasting,
a 'cat-pee aroma' is
a compliment.

Tomcat urine
smells like
cheddar cheese.

Cheese is
the most shoplifted
food in the UK.

Ⓘ

Americans eat
three times as much cheese
as they did in 1970.

Americans eat
nine times more broccoli
than they did in 1970.

1 in 8 Americans
have worked at McDonald's.

1 in 10 Americans
think HTML is
a sexually transmitted disease.

In 2011, the United Nations
declared that
access to the Internet
is a basic human right.

The original purpose
of the United Nations was
to win the Second World War.

The name 'United Nations'
was Franklin D. Roosevelt's idea.
He rushed to tell Winston Churchill,
who was towelling himself
stark naked in his bathroom.

When catering staff at the UN
went on strike in 2003,
$10,000 worth of food
and silverware
was stolen.

Q

UN Secretary-General Ban Ki-moon
celebrated his election by singing
'Ban Ki-moon Is Coming to Town'
to the tune of
'Santa Claus Is Coming to Town'.

'Santa Claus Is Coming to Town'
was first sung in November 1934.
By Christmas, it had sold
400,000 copies.

Every Christmas Day,
400,000 Britons
go out to a shop
to buy batteries.

The waste produced
at Christmas each year
in Britain would fill
400,000 double-decker buses.

Little Richard
was a washer-up
at a bus station.

Edward Elgar
was the bandmaster
in a lunatic asylum.

Leo Fender
couldn't play the guitar.

Rapper Ice-T's
real name is
Tracy Lauren Marrow.

Johnny Cash's estate
once refused permission
for his hit 'Ring of Fire' to be
used in a commercial for
haemorrhoid cream.

The original advertisement
to recruit band members
for the Village People read:
'Macho types wanted:
must have moustache.'

Coldplay
used to be called
Starfish.

Oasis
are named
after a leisure centre
in Swindon.

There are more people
living in mobile homes
in the US than live in
the whole of the Netherlands.

According to Julius Caesar,
the most civilised people in Britain
lived in Kent.

A 2011 opinion poll
found that 51% of Britons
want the reinstatement
of the death penalty.

20% of the world's CCTV
is in Britain.

Ⓘ

There are more
CCTV cameras
in the Shetland Islands
than in San Francisco.

The word 'British'
is the most common word
used by people in the UK
searching the Internet for porn.

The annual awards ceremony
of the UK porn industry
is called the SHAFTAs.

Until 1910,
film studios didn't credit actors
in case they asked for
more money.

71% of
Oscar-winners' tears
have been shed
since 1995.

Oscar Hammerstein II
is the only Oscar
ever to win
an Oscar.

Harvey Weinstein of Miramax
has been thanked
12 times at the Oscars –
once more than God.

Nigeria is
the world's third-largest
movie-producing country
but has only eight cinemas.

Luxembourg
is the only country in the world
ruled by a Grand Duke.

The appropriate response to
'How are you?'
in Luxembourgish
is '*Tip-Top*'.

The English word 'squirrel'
is particularly difficult for
Germans to pronounce.

The most difficult
tongue-twister in English is
'pad kid poured curd pulled cod'.

The giant palm salamander
can stick its tongue out
50 times faster than
you can blink.

The eyes of a giant squid
are the size of
basketballs.

90% of all jellyfish
are smaller than
a human thumbnail.

Jellyfish
born on the
Columbia space shuttle
suffered from vertigo
when they returned to Earth.

The idea that sitting
too close to the TV
is bad for your eyes
was started by a
lamp manufacturer.

René Descartes
had a fetish for
cross-eyed women.

Reindeer have
golden eyes
in summer
and blue eyes
in winter.

Rats get
more depressed
in summer than in winter.

The smell of freshly cut grass
is a plant distress call.

In 2012,
the fifth-oldest tree in the world
was burned down by a
crystal-meth addict.

The second episode
of the *The Muppets*
was called 'Sex and Violence'.

In some parts of Germany,
it is illegal to show
The Life of Brian
on Good Friday.

The first Academy Award
for Best Picture in 1927
featured an all-male kiss.

Sexmoan,
a small fishing town in the Philippines,
changed its name in 1991 to
Sasmuan.

The Lego company
was originally called
Billund Maskinsnedkeri.

By 2019, there will be
more Lego figures
on Earth than people.

There are more than
915,000,000 ways
to combine six standard
Lego bricks.

There are about
294,000,000,000,000
leaves in the world;
for every leaf
there are 340 ants.

If you feed silkworms
mulberry leaves
sprayed with pink fabric dye,
they make pink silk.

Until the 19th century,
champagne was pink
and had no bubbles.

①

UK house spiders include
the Pink Prowler, the Spitting Spider
and the Missing Sector Orb Weaver.

95% of the spiders
in your house have
never been outside.

The daddy-long-legs
flosses after meals by
pulling each of its eight legs
through its jaws.

Frogs' legs were eaten in Britain
for 7,000 years before
they were eaten
in France.

French toast
is thousands of years older
than France.

Lake Baikal in Russia
is a thousand times older
than any other lake on Earth.

If the rest of the planet's
fresh water disappeared,
there would be enough
left in Lake Baikal
to supply humanity
for 50 years.

Modern humans
evolved 80,000 years
after javelins were invented.

Anne Boleyn was
the only British monarch
beheaded with a sword.

The three Russian cosmonauts
whose spacecraft depressurised
just before re-entry in 1971 are the
only human beings to have died
outside the Earth's atmosphere.

In space you can cry
but your tears won't fall,
they just puddle up
under your eye.

If all the salt in the oceans were
spread evenly over the land,
it would be 500 feet deep.

(i)

Eels
can live inside
sharks' hearts.

Whales' vaginas
can be large enough
to walk through.

Grey whales
always mate in a threesome:
two males to one female.

Male squirrels
can perform fellatio
on themselves.

The Empress Josephine
had a pet orang-utan
that joined her for dinner
dressed in a white cotton blouse.

A salamander
can have its brain removed,
cut into slices, shuffled, minced,
put back in again and
still function as normal.

As soon as they find
a rock to anchor themselves to,
young sea squirts
eat their own brains.

Two-thirds
of an octopus's brain
is in its limbs.

A stressed or sick octopus
will sometimes bite
its own limbs off.

The world record holder
of the longest accurate
archery shot
has no arms.

In 1986, Michael Foot's appointment
as chair of a disarmament committee
prompted *The Times* headline:
'Foot Heads Arms Body'.

The body of the sea otter
has a pouch across the front
where it keeps rocks
to break open shellfish.

(i)

Louis XIV's
favourite seasoning
was soy sauce.

The volume of soy sauce
brewed in the Netherlands each year
is greater than that of all the gold
mined in human history.

In 2011, Australia minted
a giant 'A$1 million' gold coin.
It weighed over a ton
and used gold worth
A$52 million.

In 1988, there were
600,000 illegal
gold prospectors
in Brazil.

In Brazil,
'Rio' is pronounced
'Hio'.

'Dr Seuss'
should be pronounced
'Dr Zoice'.

The ancient Egyptian word for 'cat'
was pronounced
'miaow'.

Lettuce was sacred to Min,
the ancient Egyptian god of fertility,
because it grew long and straight
and oozed a milky substance
when rubbed.

Aristotle thought
small penises were better
because semen got cold
in large ones.

Ancient Greeks
declared their love for a woman
by throwing an apple at her.

Terry's used to make
a Chocolate Lemon and
a Chocolate Apple.

In 1976,
Ron Wayne,
co-founder of Apple,
sold his shares for $800;
today they would be worth
$35 billion.

James and the Giant Peach
was originally called
James and the Giant Cherry.

Twister
was originally called
Pretzel.

The Boy Scouts'
motto 'Be prepared'
was originally followed by
'to die for your country'.

Homer's epics
were originally
set to music.

Classical music
played in restaurants
increases the amount
people spend on wine.

Drinking wine
before a meal
makes you eat 25% more.

Wine drinkers
pour 12% more wine
into a glass they're holding
than one that's sitting on the table.

'Response to Those who
Criticise Me for Spending Money
on Old Wine & Prostitutes'
is a lost work by Aristippus,
a disciple of Socrates.

The ancient Greek philosopher
Heraclitus attempted to cure
a serious illness by lying in
the sun covered in cow dung.
He died the following day.

An Egyptian cure for insanity
was to eat snake meatballs
under a full moon.

In the Himalayas,
the smoke from burning millipedes
is used to treat haemorrhoids.

Queen Elizabeth I
owned two 'unicorn horns'
that were supposed to
purify water and cure sickness.

23 Nobel Prizes for Medicine
have been won as a result of
research on guinea pigs.

Eight million years ago,
guinea pigs were
the size of cows.

American cows
produce four times as much milk
as they did in 1942.

British fishermen
work 17 times harder
than they did in the 1880s,
to catch the same number of fish.

It's illegal in Saudi Arabia
for men to work
in lingerie shops.

Franz Liszt
was the first musician
to have women's underwear
thrown at him.

In 2014,
a pair of underpants
donated by the mayor of Brussels
was stolen from the
Brussels Underpants Museum.

JFK
was wearing a corset
when he was shot.

Sir Alex Ferguson
collects mementoes of
the assassination of JFK.

Hugo Chávez,
former president of Venezuela,
hosted the chat show *Aló Presidente*
every Sunday from 1999 to 2012.

Gurbanguly Berdimuhamedow,
the president of Turkmenistan,
sacked 30 TV news staff in 2008
after a cockroach was spotted
walking across the set
during a bulletin.

Susilo Bambang Yudhoyono
has released three pop-song albums
since becoming the
president of Indonesia.

The Royal Navy uses blasts of
Britney Spears's 'Oops! . . . I Did It Again'
to scare off Somali pirates.

94% of terrorist campaigns
fail to achieve a single one of
their strategic goals.

Saudi law defines atheists
as terrorists.

Saudi Arabia is considering
stopping execution by beheading
due to a shortage of
official swordsmen.

Ⓠ

At his execution,
Louis XVI was too fat
to fit into the guillotine.

Oliver Cromwell was
dug up and beheaded
two years after his death.

In 1944, nine US airmen were
shot down over Chichi Jima.
Eight of them were executed
(four of whom were also eaten)
and one (George H. W. Bush)
went on to become president.

The Red Baron's final word
was *'kaput'*.

The Red Arrows
were originally known as
the Red Pelicans.

More US Air Force pilots
are training to fly drones
than are training to fly planes.

Fighter pilots
in stressful situations
release such large amounts
of hormones that they
may ejaculate.

56% of British airline pilots admit
to having fallen asleep on the job,
and 29% say they've woken up
to find their co-pilot asleep.

(i)

A quarter of
American couples
sleep in separate beds.

The Japanese
sleep two hours
a night less than
the Chinese.

Blind people
are twice as likely to
smell things in their dreams
as sighted people.

Blind people
are four times more likely
to have nightmares
than sighted people.

In 2013, China's only female
Mao Zedong impersonator
was divorced by her husband, who
'got tired of feeling that he was
sleeping with the Chairman'.

Sleeping on your stomach
is the most likely position
to produce erotic dreams.

Duck-billed platypuses
do not have stomachs.

The eyes of the
celestial eye goldfish
really are bigger than
its stomach.

The pupils of human eyes
are at their biggest as an
adolescent and slowly
get smaller until
the age of 60.

Human brains
are 10% smaller
than they were
20,000 years ago.

Einstein's brain was
smaller than average.

In 1939, the US army
was smaller than the
armies of Portugal or Romania
and ranked 17th in the world;
by 1945, it numbered 8.3 million.

In the 1930s,
the US army drew up plans
to invade Mexico and Canada.

Alternative names proposed for
Canada in 1867 were Tuponia,
Borealia, Cabotia, Transatlantica,
Victorialand and Superior.

When Canada's Northwest Territories
were divided in two in 1999, people
voted to keep the old name.
The runner-up
was 'Bob'.

For 500 years
from the 13th century,
70% of Englishmen were called
Robert, John, Thomas, Richard
or William.

252 people
are born every
minute.

'Last shake o' the bag'
was Victorian slang for
'youngest child'.

When having their photograph taken,
Victorians said 'prunes'
rather than 'cheese'
to make themselves
look more serious.

When Danes pose for photos,
they say 'orange', the Chinese say
'aubergine' and the Germans
say 'ant shit'.

There are beetles
named after Darth Vader,
Kate Winslet and Adolf Hitler.

Nachos
were invented by a man
named Nacho.

Men whose initials
have positive connotations,
like LOV or WIN,
live 4½ years longer
than those with negative ones,
like BAD or PIG.

In 1883, a man named Jack Ferry
crossed the English Channel
on a floating tricycle.

The father of Jeff Bezos,
founder of Amazon,
was a unicyclist in a circus.

There are 100,000
more bicycles in Amsterdam
than there are people.

In 2009,
a search of Loch Ness
for the Loch Ness monster
located 100,000
golf balls.

At any one time
there are 100,000
ships at sea.

The world's largest
container ships can carry
746 million bananas.

Bananas
are considered unlucky
on fishing boats.

In 1923,
the sheet music for
'Yes, We Have No Bananas'
sold 1,000 copies a day.

There are more than
1,000 species of banana.
We eat only one of them.

Eating
20 million bananas
would give you a fatal dose
of radioactivity.

Bananas
are used to make
kimonos.

Queen Victoria
had a novelty bustle
with a music box that played
'God Save the Queen'
when she sat down.

The 'Masters in Lunacy'
were Victorian officials who
investigated whether people
claiming to be insane
were faking it.

When he enlisted in the army,
J. R. R. Tolkien's son Michael
put down his father's profession
as 'Wizard'.

New Zealand
has an official
National Wizard.

The New Zealand badminton team
was nicknamed 'the Black Cocks',
but had to drop it after complaints.

New Zealand's 90-Mile Beach
is 55 miles long.

Over the last 10,000 years
Niagara Falls has moved
seven miles upstream.

The United States
doubled in size in 1983,
when the Reagan administration
expanded its coastal waters
from three to 200 nautical miles.

In 2011, scientists
re-measured Norway's
beaches, islands and fjords,
adding 11,000 miles
to its coastline.

The coastline of Norway
is long enough to
circle the planet
2½ times.

Every year,
Iceland gets wider
by two centimetres.

Iceland
has 25 puffins
for every person.

Men
outnumber
women
in Vatican City
by 17 to 1.

There are as many bacteria
in two servings of yoghurt
as there are people on Earth.

The ice lost in
Antarctica every year
would be enough to give
each person on Earth
1,360,000 ice cubes.

The technical name for
an ice-cream headache is
sphenopalatine ganglioneuralgia.

Hellenologophobia
is the fear of Greek terms.

A *musophobist*
is a person who
distrusts poetry.

'Invictus',
Nelson Mandela's favourite poem,
was written by the man who
inspired the character of
Long John Silver.

80% of pirates
caught by the
European Union's
naval police
are released.

People who pirate music
also buy more legal music
than those who don't.

Barry Manilow's No. 1 hit
'I Write the Songs'
wasn't written by
Barry Manilow.

When the Arctic Monkeys formed,
none of them could play
a musical instrument.

The real
Maria von Trapp
wasn't invited to the premiere
of *The Sound of Music.*

The Duke of Wellington
played cricket for
Ireland.

The current
Earl of Sandwich
runs a chain of
sandwich shops called
Earl of Sandwich.

If you ate in a
different New York eatery
every day for 12 years,
you still wouldn't have visited
all of the city's restaurants.

25 November 2012 was
the first day since 1960 that
there was no murder
or manslaughter in
New York City.

During its restoration in 1982,
the Statue of Liberty's head
was accidentally installed
two feet off-centre.

New buildings in New York
must have twice as many
women's toilets as men's.

Toilet Duck, cellophane
and the division sign (÷)
were all invented
in Switzerland.

The first sketch
for the design of the Mini
was drawn on a napkin
in Switzerland.

Switzerland monitors
its airspace around the clock
but only intercepts illegal flights
during office hours.

In 2006,
the most popular name for
cows in Switzerland
was Fiona.

A cow with a name
will produce 450 more
pints of milk a year than
one without a name.

The guts of
250,000 cows
were used to make
the balloon lining
for every Zeppelin.

The Spanish for
'when pigs fly' is
'when hens piss'.

In German,
things don't
'sell like hot cakes',
they 'go like warm rolls'.

German mothers-to-be
have 'roast dinners' not 'buns'
in their 'ovens'.

Pregnant women
are 42% more likely
to be in a car crash
but less likely to die
than men of the same age.

Only two countries
have not ratified
the UN Convention on
the Rights of the Child:
Somalia and the US.

The US, Papua New Guinea,
Swaziland, Liberia and Lesotho
are the only countries without
mandatory maternity leave.

A *lully-prigger* was
an 18th-century thief
who caught children and
stole their clothing.

By the time they are eight
children have forgotten
60% of what happened
before they were three.

In 1922,
Ernest Hemingway's wife
lost his entire life's work
by leaving it on a train.

In 1989, a Russian psychic
was run over by a train and killed
while attempting to prove
he could stop one using
the power of his mind.

American tank crews
have a superstition that will
not allow them to eat apricots,
allow apricots on board or even
say the word 'apricot'.

The crunch
of a crisp or an apple
in your mouth
is a mini sonic boom.

Polo mints
release light
when you
snap them.

Mice
can't see
red light.

Pregreening
is creeping forward
while waiting for a
red light to change.

Herds of sheep
moved at night must have
a white light at the front
and a red light at the rear.

Coyotes in the US
have learnt how traffic lights work
so they can cross the road safely.

Traffic lights
were introduced
18 years before
the car was invented.

In 1990, there were
no roundabouts in the US;
today there are more than 3,000.

40% of
pedestrian-crossing buttons
in Manchester
don't work.

A group of pigeons
regularly boards
the London Underground
at Hammersmith and alights
at Ladbroke Grove.

The average London pigeon
has 1.6 feet.

Deliveries by pigeon post
during the Second World War
were 95% successful.

In 1910,
the average Briton
sent 116 items by post.

The longest letter
ever printed in *The Times*
was 11,071 words long.
Today, the whole letters page
carries only 2,000 words.

84% of writers to
the letters page of *The Times*
are men.

During his lifetime
Lewis Carroll wrote
98,721 letters.

Philip Larkin and Kingsley Amis
signed off letters to each other
with the word 'bum'.

Chimpanzees
can identify each other
by looking at photographs
of their bottoms.

People can recognise
each other 90% of the time
just from the way they walk.

To perfect
Hercule Poirot's walk,
actor David Suchet
clasped a coin
between his buttocks.

Lizards
can't breathe and walk
at the same time.

Salamanders
can hear with their
lungs.

Lobsters
listen with their
legs.

A lobster's brain
is in its throat.

The human brain
cannot feel pain.

When neuroscientist James Fallon
studied the brain scans of murderers
using his own scan as a control,
he discovered he was a psychopath.

John F. Kennedy's brain
was removed during his autopsy
and is still missing.

9,000 books
are listed as missing
from the British Library.

Lee Harvey Oswald
still owes an overdue book –
The Shark and the Sardines
by Juan José Arévalo –
to Dallas public library.

Cleopatra wrote a book
about make-up.

50,000 Korans
are buried in the
mountains of Pakistan,
each one in a white shroud.

65%
of Pakistani soldiers have
dandruff.

13%
of Greek children have
dimpled cheeks.

85%
of the exhibits in
Peru's Museum of Gold
are fakes.

90%
of the thermostats
in American offices
don't work.

Davy Crockett
was a US congressman.

Whoopi Goldberg
used to be a bricklayer.

Jerry Springer
was born in Highgate
Tube station.

Phil Collins
divorced his second wife
by fax.

Q

Nobody knows
how big Pluto is.

If you stood on the
Martian equator at noon,
it would feel like
summer at your feet
and winter at your head.

From 2000 BC to AD 1992,
astronomers discovered
three new planets.
In 2014, 700 were found
in a single day.

The notebooks of
US astronauts were
fireproofed with seaweed
from the Isle of Lewis.

When the Lewis Chessmen
were discovered in 1831,
the man who found them ran away,
terrified he'd interrupted
an assembly of elves.

Dublin is home to
Ireland's National
Leprechaun Museum.

All the chickens' eggs
produced in the world each year
would make an omelette
the size of Northern Ireland.

Hummingbirds lay eggs
the size of peas.

Seahorses
beat their fins
almost as fast as
hummingbirds
beat their wings.

The Milky Way
gives birth to a new star
every 50 days.

Almost 1%
of American mothers
claim to have been virgins
when they gave birth.

The closer a woman
is to the equator,
the more likely she is to
give birth to a girl.

Newborn babies
of both sexes can
produce milk.

Flor de Guia cheese
from the Canary Islands
must only be made by women,
otherwise it is not considered
the genuine article.

Britons are
the most lactose-tolerant people
in the world.

'Cheesy'
originally meant
'excellent'.

The word 'suffragette'
started out as an insult
coined by the *Daily Mail*.

'Bingo'
was first used as slang for
'brandy'.

Charlotte Brontë was
the first person to use the terms
'cottage-garden', 'raised eyebrow',
'Now, now!', 'kitchen chair'
and 'Wild West'.

'Sexpert', 'cushty', 'freebie'
'makeover', 'comfort zone'
and 'dream team'
all date from the 1920s.

Broomstacking
is a traditional drink
taken after a game of curling;
the losing team foots the bill.

After the first recorded
hurling match
the losing team was
brutally murdered.

In 1920, Clarence Blethen
retired hurt from a baseball match
after biting himself on the bottom
with the false teeth he kept
in his back pocket.

Louis X and Charles VIII of France
both died as a result of
playing tennis.

After the Battle of Hastings,
King Harold's body was identified
by the tattoo of his wife's name
over his heart.

90% of the men in Paraguay
died in the War of the Triple Alliance.
From 1864 to 1870 they fought
Brazil, Uruguay and Argentina
simultaneously.

A refereeing decision
in a football match between
Argentina and Peru in 1964
led to a riot in which
300 fans were killed.

A fight between chameleons
is more likely to be started by
the one with brighter stripes.

The 10-spot ladybird
has between 0 and 15 spots.

William Buckland was expelled
from the shrine of St Rosalia,
patron saint of Palermo, Sicily,
for pointing out that her bones
were actually those of a goat.

Vultures can turn
a dead body into a
skeleton in under
five hours.

A walrus's
penis bone
is as long as a
human thigh bone.

There are at least
600 men in the world
with two penises.

The penis of the
Argonaut mollusc
snaps off during sex:
it can only mate
once.

Chinese eunuchs
kept their testicles in a jar
in the hope they will
reattach themselves
in the next world.

The world has
two earthquakes
every minute.

The Northern Hemisphere
is 1.5°C hotter than
the Southern Hemisphere.

90% of people live
in the Northern Hemisphere.

Wherever
a leaf is in the world,
its internal temperature
is always 21°C.

When it gets too hot,
some cacti move underground
to cool down.

Prisoners on Alcatraz
always had hot showers so
they didn't get acclimatised
to cold water and try to
escape by swimming.

In Inuit languages,
the closest word to 'freedom'
is *annakpok*, which means
'not caught'.

In the French Revolution,
prisoners were taken to the
guillotine on wagons used
to transport manure.

Scatomancy
is telling the future
by looking at turds.

Henry VIII's lavatory
at Hampton Court was known as
'The Great House of Easement'.

Predicting the death
of Henry VIII was
punishable by death.

The bell rung to mark the death
of Ivan the Terrible's son Dmitri
was tried for treason, found guilty
and exiled to Siberia.

The drugs used
for a lethal injection in Texas
cost $83.

In 2013,
Detroit stopped
issuing death certificates
because it ran out of paper.

In 2013,
the Venezuelan government
accused the opposition of
hoarding toilet paper and
causing a national shortage.

12% of a
sloth's energy
is used to climb
up and down trees
to go to the lavatory.

A single sloth
can be home to
980 different beetles.

Your kitchen sink harbours
100,000 times more germs
than your toilet bowl.

There are 20 million
sea containers in the world.
The ships' crews have no idea
what is in them.

'The Just Missed It Club'
was for people who almost
sailed on the *Titanic*.
Two weeks after it sank,
it had 118,337 members.

Jenny, the ship's cat
on the *Titanic*, did not
survive the sinking.

Over 200 mice are reported in
the Houses of Parliament each year,
but the authorities won't get a cat
because no one can be trusted
to look after it responsibly.

According to his wife Mary,
Abraham Lincoln's hobby
was cats.

Édouard Manet's cat
was eaten during
the Siege of Paris in 1870.

Karl Lagerfeld's cat has
two maids who write down
everything it does
in a special book.

During the 1741 General Election,
angry voters pelted candidates
with dead cats and dogs.

69% of the cocaine
sold in the US contains
de-worming medication.

During the Vietnam War,
each US soldier took 40
amphetamine tablets a year.

The phrase 'pipe dream'
originates from the fantasies
induced by smoking opium.

There are more
marijuana dispensaries
in Denver, Colorado,
than there are branches
of Starbucks.

Because of its Happy Meals,
McDonald's is the world's largest
distributor of toys.

The first McDonald's
only sold hot dogs.

In 2002,
the US military developed
a sandwich that stays fresh
for three years.

Human rights
were invented
in Iran.

Vegetarian sausages were
first patented in Britain in 1918,
by the future German chancellor,
Konrad Adenauer.

If they don't care
about something,
Germans say,
'It's sausage to me.'

Rice Krispies
in Germany go
'Knisper! Knasper! Knusper!'

At the end of
the Second World War,
US censors kept the news of
Germany's unconditional surrender
secret from the public for 11 hours.

The *Hindenburg* airship
was almost named
the *Hitler*.

When the *Hindenburg* exploded,
62 of the 97 passengers survived.

80% of people who are
struck by lightning
survive.

A single lightning bolt
produces enough energy
to power a family home
for a month.

The energy released by
a bolt of lightning is about
the same as that stored in
30 gallons of petrol.

The energy needed
to manufacture a new car
is equivalent to
260 gallons of petrol.

Forest fires
can be sparked by sunlight
magnified by water on
dried-out leaves.

The 45-foot long V2 rocket
carried enough alcohol to make
66,130 dry martinis.

Pee Cola
is a popular soft drink
in Ghana.

In China,
Burger King sells
PooPoo Smoothies.

The word for 'carp'
in Montenegro
is *krap*.

Barf
is Persian for
'snow'.

The snow at the South Pole
reflects sound so well
you can hear people
talking a mile away.

The first snow goggles
were made of slices of
polished caribou antler.

Icebergs
make a crackling sound
known as 'bergy seltzer'.

The world's largest iceberg
set off from Antarctica in 2000.
It was larger than Jamaica and
parts of it still haven't melted.

The world's largest
and most complete
Tyrannosaurus rex skeleton
is called Sue.

Britain's largest pig
is called Boris. He contains
enough pork to make
6,000 sausages.

The largest lizard
in Australia
can run as fast as
Usain Bolt.

@

AKB48,
Japan's largest pop group,
has 89 members.

Japan has twice as many
bank holidays as the UK,
including 'Greenery Day' and
'Respect for the Aged Day'.

In 18th-century America,
Thanksgiving was celebrated
with a day of fasting and prayer.

In 2013,
Hanukkah and Thanksgiving
began on the same day.
The next time this will happen
will be in AD 79811.

In the year 20860,
the Islamic and Christian calendars
will finally agree.

According to
the Mayan calendar,
the next time the
'world is going to end'
is 3 May 7138.

There is a 12% chance
that a game of Monopoly
will go on indefinitely.

If you exposed
a diamond on a sunbed,
it would eventually evaporate,
but you wouldn't notice any change
for 10 billion years.

On 28 June 2009,
Stephen Hawking hosted a party
for time travellers from the future.
Nobody showed up.

Black holes
are not black.

Robins' 'red' breasts
are orange.

Ripe limes
are yellow.

Guinness
isn't black;
it's very dark red.

Guinness
isn't suitable
for vegetarians;
it contains traces
of fish bladder.

Human teeth
evolved from
fish scales.

Fish
don't need to
learn how to swim
in schools.

By tapping canes,
stamping feet and
making clicking sounds,
humans can learn to
echolocate like bats.

Species of bat include
the wrinkle-faced bat,
the thumbless bat,
the Antillean ghost-faced bat,
the flower-faced bat and
the big-eared woolly bat.

Without bats
there would be no tequila.
It's made from the agave plant,
which is pollinated by bats.

Tequila heated to 800°C
can be made into diamonds.

Moss Cider
is a drink made from
apples grown in
Manchester's Moss Side.

Grapples
are apples that
taste like grapes.

Grapes
are poisonous to
dogs.

Avocados
are toxic to
horses.

Ⓠ

Philip
is Greek for
'horse-lover'.

Falling in love
costs you, on average,
two close friends.

Valentine's Day
is banned in
Iran, Malaysia, Saudi Arabia
and Uzbekistan.

More than 5,000 Swedish men
have the first name Love.

There are
60 people in Venezuela
whose first name is Hitler.

The place where
Hitler killed himself
is now a children's playground.

In ancient Rome,
fathers had the legal right
to kill their children.

In J. M. Barrie's novel,
Peter Pan ruthlessly
'thinned out' the Lost Boys
when they got too old.

In the winter of 1918,
half the children in Berlin
were suffering from rickets.

The population of Ireland
is still smaller than it was
before the Great Famine
of 1845.

The labourers who built
the Great Wall of China were
were fed on sauerkraut.

Before eating,
Nikola Tesla,
the 'father of electricity',
polished each piece of cutlery
with 18 napkins.

Ancient Romans
ate puppies.

Eating dogs
is legal in
44 US states.

2.8 million
American dogs
are on antidepressants.

Babies
can hear
dog whistles.

Dog yawns
are infectious.

You can tell if
someone is yawning
from their eyes alone.

No one knows
why we yawn.

Hamsters blink
one eye at a time.

Hamsters can store
half their own weight in food
in their cheeks.

Tomato frogs
secrete a glue that
causes a predator's lips
to stick together.

By the time they
leave high school
American children
will have eaten 1,500
peanut-butter-and-jelly
sandwiches.

Alan Shepard took
a peanut to the Moon.
When he brought it back,
Steve McQueen tried to eat it.

Astronauts' hearts
become rounder
in space.

Astronaut
Harrison Schmitt
is allergic to
the Moon.

Astronaut
John Young smuggled
a corned-beef sandwich
into space.

A third of British
office workers have
the same thing for
lunch every day.

British families
throw away the equivalent
of six meals a week.

Britons spend
eight times as long
watching television
as they do cooking meals.

In spite of all
the cookery shows
on British television,
the average Briton
only knows four recipes.

There is a variety of carrot
beginning with every letter
of the alphabet except X.

Vegetables are four times
healthier than fruit.

Corn, avocados,
cucumbers, peas,
beans and peppers
are fruits, not
vegetables.

A quarter
of all the vegetables
eaten in the US are
French fries.

The Aztecs
wore necklaces
made of popcorn.

Unpopped
popcorn kernels
are called 'old maids'
or 'spinsters'.

A 'singlewoman'
was medieval slang
for a prostitute.

88% of women
routinely wear shoes
that are too small
for their feet.

British feet
have grown by
two shoe sizes
in the last 40 years.

Our little toes
were much stronger
before shoes became
widespread.

In 1967,
Picoazá, Ecuador, elected
a brand of foot deodorant
as the town's mayor.

New research shows that,
for luxury brands,
the ruder the sales staff,
the higher the sales.

Jaguars
are attracted by
Calvin Klein's
Obsession for Men.

Termites
like the smell
of biro ink.

An Atlantic salmon's
sense of smell is 1,000 times
better than a dog's.

There are
one billion dogs
in the world.

Every day,
the human body makes
300 billion new cells,
three times as many as there are
galaxies in the universe.

NASA estimates that
the near-Earth asteroid, Eros,
contains 20 billion tons of gold.

The opening ceremony
of the Beijing Olympics
was the first time a billion people
have watched a sporting event.

At the 1932 Olympics,
the 3,000-metre steeplechase
was run over 3,400 metres
because an official lost count
of the number of laps.

ⓘ

Croquet was dropped
as an Olympic sport after 1900
because only one spectator
turned up to watch.

The first man to swim from
John O'Groats to Land's End
grew a beard to protect his face
from jellyfish stings.

Each person in a swimming pool
leaves behind
between 8 and 20
teaspoonfuls of urine.

3,079
chemical compounds
have been identified
in human urine.

Virtually all Koreans
lack the gene that
produces smelly armpits.

The tobacco hornworm
uses its terrible breath
to fend off predators.

Enough Polo mints
are produced in one year
to give everyone in the UK
114 each.

The first
commercial chewing gum
was made from
spruce-tree resin.

Only 1% of a tree
is actually alive.

The mortality rate
of pop stars is 1.7 times
higher than the average.

One in nine
Honduran men
will be murdered.

Boys in Bronze Age Russia
had to slay their own dogs
to prove they were ready
to become warriors.

There are more
Internet hosts in Manhattan
than there are in
the whole of Africa.

88% of working adults
in sub-Saharan Africa
don't have a bank account.

Charitable donations
of clothing to Africa
have led to the collapse
of its textile industry.

40 million tons of dust
are blown from the Sahara
to the Amazon every year.

Lebanon is the only country
in Africa or the Middle East
that doesn't have a desert.

The only desert
in Britain is
Dungeness Nature Reserve
in Kent.

Everyone on Palmerston Island,
in the middle of the Pacific,
speaks with a
Gloucestershire accent.

Accents in Britain
change noticeably
every 25 miles.

Scotland
has the largest bog
in Europe.

There are more
stretch limos in Glasgow
than in Los Angeles.

There are more
Catholics in Scotland
than in Northern Ireland.

In 2007, Scotland
spent £125,000 devising
a new national slogan.
The winning entry was:
'Welcome to Scotland.'

In 2013,
6,000 papal medals were
withdrawn by the Vatican
after it was found they
read 'Lesus' instead
of 'Jesus'.

'Bird'
was originally spelled
brid.

'Empty'
was originally spelled
emty.

'Misspell'
is one of the most
commonly misspelled words
in the English language.

The number '2'
is known by 42% of
Slovenian two-year-olds
but only 4% of
English two-year-olds.

The word 'twelve'
is worth 12 points
in Scrabble.

Moving
each letter of the word 'yes'
16 places further up the alphabet
produces the word '*oui*'.

The words 'ace, two, three,
four, five, six, seven, eight,
nine, ten, jack, queen, king'
contain 52 letters.

The largest known
prime number is
17 million digits long.

The longest English word
with all its letters in
alphabetical order is 'Aegilops',
a flowering grass
whose name means
'a herb liked by goats'.

Google and Yahoo
both use goats to
trim their lawns.

Goats
can't cry.

If you tickle a rat every day,
it'll start laughing
as soon as it sees you.

Rats
can feel regret.

Being lonely is
as bad for your health as
smoking 15 cigarettes a day.

There are enough
viruses on Earth
to fill 150
Super Bowl stadiums.

The first Cannes Film Festival
closed after only one night
due to the outbreak of
the Second World War.

In the Second World War,
Ribena was such an important
source of vitamin C that two
fake Ribena factories were built
to confuse German bombers.

During the Second World War,
Lucozade was made
from conkers.

During the Second World War,
the Polish army recruited
a bear called Wojtek,
a name that means
'he who enjoys war'.

In 1384,
a 10-year-old Hungarian girl
called Hedwig
was crowned
King of Poland.

Offa's Dyke
was built 200 years before
King Offa was born.

Cleopatra's Needle
was 1,000 years old when
Cleopatra was born.

Seven US presidents
were born
in log cabins.

For the last
three months of his life,
US President James Garfield
had to be fed everything
through his anus.

George H. W. Bush
wears socks with
his own face on.

The first armoured
presidential car was
a Cadillac that had
previously belonged
to Al Capone.

In 1924,
half the cars
in the world were
Fords.

Half the world's cork
comes from
Portugal.

In Sweden,
a Chinese burn
is known as the
'thousand-needle prank'.

A man in China
hired virtual assassins
to kill his son's
World of Warcraft character
so he'd stop playing.

In 2013,
police in the Maldives
arrested a coconut
on suspicion of vote rigging.

In 2007,
police in Iran
detained 14 squirrels
suspected of spying.

In 2012,
the New Zealand government
took legal action to prevent
a couple calling their child
Anal.

In the Norwegian town
of Longyearbyen,
it is illegal to die.

In 17th-century Virginia,
missing three Sunday Masses in a row
carried the death penalty.

In 19th-century Maryland,
it was illegal to
sell mineral water
on a Sunday.

In Singapore,
it's illegal to
use a public lavatory
and not flush it.

A 1571 law stated that
all Englishmen must wear
knitted hats on Sundays.

In 2013, a judge in Michigan
found himself in contempt of court
when his mobile phone went off
during a trial.

Pasta
is Spanish for
'money'.

'Trampoline' comes from
the Spanish for
'diving board'.

It is possible
to travel by zip wire
from Spain to Portugal.

For 14 years
during the Napoleonic wars,
the capital of Portugal was
Rio de Janeiro.

Tempura
was introduced to Japan
by Portuguese missionaries
in the 16th century.

George Washington
is worshipped as a god
by Japanese Shinto priests
in Hawaii.

Harold Wilson
was so poor when he
was at university that
his mother sent him
meat in the post.

Nick Clegg
once did community service for
setting fire to a rare cactus collection
while drunk on a school trip.

The world's tallest statue,
currently being built in India,
is of a deputy prime minister.

A third of adults in India
play chess at least once a week.

Indians read
twice as much
as Britons.

The average Briton
has read fewer than half
the books they own.

Haile Gebrselassie,
the Ethiopian distance runner,
ran six miles to and from
school each day. He still runs
with a crook in his arm,
as if he's carrying his books.

The Persians
invented horse-riding
and trousers.

Mozart kept
a fart diary.

1 in 6
Google searches
have never been
searched for before.

A 'googolplex' is a number
so vast it can't be written down:
there's not enough room
in the universe for
all the zeros.

Google employees
are encouraged to use
a fifth of their time at work
on their own non-Google projects.

Everyone has at least
50,000 thoughts a day but
95% of them are the same
as the day before.

Three-quarters of Britons
have a drawer at home
full of miscellaneous junk.

At the Vancouver Winter Olympics,
the medals were made from
recycled televisions and
computer circuit boards.

Azodicarbonamide
is a chemical compound that
makes things softer and bouncier,
including yoga mats, flip-flops and
the buns in Big Macs.

Dry cleaning was invented when
someone knocked over a
kerosene lamp and noticed it
removed stains from their clothes.

It's impossible
to set fire to a pool of petrol
by throwing a lit cigarette into it.

The US Patent Office
insisted on proof that the
Ouija board worked before
granting the patent in 1891.

To save lives,
Volvo gave away the patent
for its seatbelt.

One in four people
killed on British roads were
not wearing seatbelts.

You are four times more likely
to drown in your bath
than you are to die
of food poisoning.

95% of people don't wash
their hands properly
before leaving a
public toilet.

Japanese companies advertise on
packs of tissues given out free at
train stations, because the toilets
there often don't have loo paper.

People with higher incomes
generally prefer their loo paper
to unravel over the roll,
while those with lower incomes
prefer it to go under.

In the Second World War,
British troops were issued with
three sheets of toilet paper a day;
American soldiers got 22.

Jack Kerouac
typed his novel *On the Road*
on a 120-foot roll of paper
in three weeks.

According to the
India Book of Records,
the longest garland
made of cattle dung
was 1¼ miles long.

Modern fishing lines
can be up to
75 miles long.

The 3.4 million coins
in the longest-ever
line of coins stretched
for over 40 miles.

The first coin
minted in the US
bore the slogan
'Mind Your Business'.

In the Great Depression,
old tyres and fish skin
were used as money in the US.

Two-thirds
of all $100 bills
are held outside the US.

$1,200,000,000,000 of
US money is in circulation,
but nobody knows
where 85% of it is.

Most people walk 12 steps
carrying a piece of litter
before they drop it.

400 million gallons of raw sewage
flow out of New York every year;
the same as the volume of petrol
Americans use every day.

Mexican households
generate 30% more rubbish
than American households.

Sweden is
so good at recycling
that it has run out of rubbish
and imports 80,000 tons a year
from Norway.

Sweden
makes biofuel
from dead rabbits.

Pope Gregory I
declared rabbit foetuses
were marine animals
and could be eaten
during Lent.

Pope Francis I
used to work as a bouncer
in a Buenos Aires nightclub.

The Greek god Atlas
had an aunt
called Doris.

(i)

Abraham Lincoln
failed five times to get elected
to Congress and the Senate
before being elected president.

In 80% of
US presidential elections
the taller candidate has won.

The Somali word for 'president'
also means 'big head',
and the candidate with
the biggest head
usually wins.

If a Hong Kong
election ends in a tie,
the candidates draw from a bag
of numbered ping-pong balls.

Five years before
he won Wimbledon,
Fred Perry was
world table-tennis champion.

Before he became a spy,
John le Carré washed elephants
for the Swiss National Circus.

Before he became president,
Bashar al-Assad was head of
the Syrian Computer Club.

In 2013, a mobile-phone app
allowing Azerbaijanis to track
the presidential election reported
the president's massive victory
24 hours before the polls opened.

To be *appstracted*
is to be distracted
by an app.

The French equivalent
of LOL is MDR:
mort de rire – dead from laughing.

The 1989 article that proposed
the acronym LOL
also suggested using
'H' to mean 'Huh?'

The word 'huh' is understood
in all known languages.

Hawaiian, Icelandic and Zulu
have given more words to English
than Welsh or Cornish.

When Columbus
'discovered' the New World,
there were at least 50 million people
living in the Americas.

Before humans reached Hawaii,
the dominant animals there
were giant ducks.

At the 1928 Olympics,
oarsman Henry Pearce stopped to let
a family of ducks cross his lane
and went on to win the gold medal.

At the 1956 Olympics,
Russian rower Vyacheslav Ivanov
was so excited at winning gold that
he dropped his medal into the lake
and it was never found.

Toshers were
men who earned a living by
searching London's sewers
for lost valuables.

People in India
panning for gold in sewers
make four times the average wage.

'You have a turd in your teeth'
was a common insult in
17th-century England.

The terms
'Tory', 'Labour'
and 'Prime Minister'
all began as insults.

The House of Lords
has a rifle range
in the basement.

Membership of
the Conservative Party
has fallen by 97%
since the 1950s.

The surname Cameron
means 'crooked mouth'.

The facial expressions
on Lego figures
have become increasingly angry
over the last 30 years.

A 'rough and tumble'
was originally a boxing bout
without any rules.

In the 1890s,
Samoan cricket matches
had teams of up to 150 a side
and lasted for over a fortnight.

Clinton, Montana,
holds an annual testicle festival.
Known as Testy Fest, it includes
Ball Eating, Miss TestyFest,
Itty Bitty Titty, Mr Fun Buns
and Nicest Arms.

A manatee's nipples
are in its armpits.

Despite producing milk,
neither the platypus nor the echidna
have nipples.

Humans
are the only primates
with permanent
breasts.

The largest
bra size is
48V.

Male
Dayak fruit bats
lactate.

Breast milk is
a laxative.

Women's breast tissue
ages faster than the
rest of their
bodies.

Victorian slang
for breasts was
'Cupid's kettledrums'.

Q

People
are more likely
to co-operate with you
if you give them something
warm to hold.

Koalas
hug trees
to keep cool.

Spider silk
conducts heat
better than most metals.

Spiders
seem bigger
the more scared
you are.

1 in 6 Americans
over seven feet tall are
professional basketball players.

Joseph Goebbels
was the same height
as Lindsay Lohan.

In the 1980s,
Hollywood planned
a version of *Doctor Who*,
starring Michael Jackson
as the Doctor.

The Daleks
were based on
the Nazis.

Ⓠ

In 2001,
Southend-on-Sea had to redesign
its new traffic-warden outfits
when it was pointed out they were
emblazoned with the letters 'SS'.

The first time
Hitler and Mussolini met,
Mussolini described Hitler as a
'mad little clown'.

The clown
Joseph Grimaldi
was seen by 1 in 8 people
in Victorian London.

Charles Dickens's son Francis
was a Canadian Mountie
for 12 years.

Canada
banned baby walkers
in 2004.

Pay toilets
were banned in Chicago
in 1974.

Skateboards
were banned in Norway
between 1978 and 1989.

In 1948,
a single law in Spain
banned blasphemy,
wood-chopping
and keeping poultry.

There was a law
in Sparta against having an
unmanly complexion.

King Archidamus of Sparta
was fined for marrying a short wife
because officials believed she
would give birth to 'kinglets'
rather than kings.

The jockey Frankie Dettori
is four inches shorter
than rugby player Tom Youngs,
but only half his weight.

People eating in a
group of seven or more
eat twice as much as
people eating alone.

A newborn blue whale
puts on 14 stone
every day.

Whales can't
taste anything
but salt.

Full-fat milk
contains only
3.5% fat.

A one-year-old baby
is 30% fat.

A newborn baby
sucks in air with
50 times the power
of an adult.

Over your life,
you take 850 million
breaths.

Potato aphids
will not have sex
if they detect a drop
in air pressure.

The 'soul-sucking' wasp,
Ampulex dementor,
is named after the
Dementors in *Harry Potter*
because of the way it
paralyses cockroaches.

The oldest-known
parasitic worm
was found protruding
from the backside of a
25-million-year-old cockroach.

A nematode worm's brain
is shaped like
a doughnut.

Penis worms
do not have heads
(or penises).

Beetles
don't have
taste buds.

Adult burying beetles
punish offspring
who nag for food
by eating them.

Ancient Egyptian bakers
who cheated their customers
were punished by having their ear
nailed to the door of the bakery.

The English word 'dinner'
comes from the French word *disner*,
meaning 'breakfast'.

In Hindi,
a *chummery*
is a house shared by
two or more bachelors.

In Geoffrey Chaucer's time,
a 'cockney' meant
a spoiled child.

In the Middle Ages,
the word 'comical'
meant 'epileptic'.

The longest bout of
hiccups lasted
67 years.

In the 15th century,
English 'sweating sickness'
killed thousands of people
and then disappeared;
nobody knows what it was.

Periwinkles
are used to cure
leukaemia.

In Greece
between 1920 and 1983,
leprosy was
grounds for divorce.

In 2013,
the US Navy recorded
its first case of scurvy
since the Civil War.

In Nelson's navy,
it took 2,000 mature oak trees
to build a 74-gun ship.

The
modern Spanish Navy
is still called
the *Armada*.

In spite of
'women and children first',
men have been twice as likely
as women to survive
shipwrecks since 1852.

St Lucia is the only
country in the world
named after a woman.

Rome
has 7,575 streets
named after men
but only 580 after
women.

Q

59 of the 60
oldest living people
are women.

The oldest person
in the world dies,
on average,
every 8 months.

The oldest you can be
to go on a
Club 18–30 holiday
is 35.

A quarter of
unmarried Japanese
30-year-olds
are still virgins.

More than
50,000 people in Japan
are over 100 years old.

The average
Japanese farmer
is 70 years old.

A common form of
public apology in Japan
is shaving one's head.

Most Britons say 'sorry'
almost two million times
in their lives.

The first football rulebook
in Argentina stated that
a player who had been fouled
could accept an apology
rather than involve the referee.

Argentinians
speak Spanish with
a strong Italian accent.

In Washington DC,
the Slovakian and Slovenian
embassies meet once a month to
exchange wrongly addressed mail.

Slovenian men do
twice as much housework
as Italian men.

80% of Italians
aged between 18 and 30
live with their parents.

If Prince Charles
becomes king, he will be
the oldest monarch
ever crowned
in Britain.

Prince Charles
runs his car on biofuel
made from wine.

Wine can be 'aged'
by passing it through
an electric field
for three minutes.

A £5 bottle of wine
tastes better if you've paid
£45 for it.

If food prices
had risen at the same rate
as house prices over the last 40 years,
a loaf of bread would cost
£4.87.

33% of the bread
produced in the UK is wasted,
compared with 6% of
the alcohol.

Alcohol costs 60% more
in the UK than
it does in France.

20 million barrels of whisky
are maturing in warehouses
in Scotland.

In 14th-century England,
children were
baptised in cider.

Wayne Rooney's
voicemail password
was 'Stella Artois'.

1 in 10 passwords
used on the Internet
are either 'Password',
or '123456' or '12345678'.

The least common
PIN number
is 8068.

Alternative names
considered for Twitter were
FriendStalker and
Throbber.

85% of Twitter's content
comes from
15% of users.

Half of all tweets
are pointless babble.

One-third of
the population of China
can't speak the country's
official language.

Only a fifth
of the Sahara desert
is sand.

At least a tenth
of the population of Mauritania
are slaves.

Mississippi
didn't prohibit slavery
until 1995.

The Tightwad Bank
serves the town of
Tightwad, Missouri.

Two-thirds
of all bankruptcies in the US
are caused by medical bills.

More than 80,000
bartenders in America
have university degrees.

As a nuclear-safety inspector,
Homer Simpson earns
$20,000 more than
the average American.

Americans today
work for the equivalent of
one month more each year
than they did in 1976.

There is a French law
that stops people
answering work emails
after 6 p.m.

Apple Inc.
is worth more than
Sweden, Poland or Nigeria.

The founders of Hewlett-Packard
flipped a coin to decide
which of them would come first
in the company name.

Facebook is cited
in one-third of
UK divorce cases.

A survey in Britain in 1943
found that the top tip for a
successful marriage was
'liking' your partner.

The Nobel Prize-winning novelist
Gabriel García Márquez
was married for 55 years.
Every day his wife Mercedes put
a yellow rose on his desk.

The first person
to go over Niagara Falls
in a barrel and survive was
a 63-year-old widow.

Hurricanes
with female names
are deadlier than ones
named after men.

All New Mexico
whiptail lizards
are female.

The German phrase
Eierlegende Wollmilchsau,
literally, 'egg-laying wool-milk-sow',
describes a woman who
can do anything.

In Saudi Arabia,
it is illegal for women
to enter hospitals
unaccompanied by men.

Saudi Arabia
has an official
anti-witchcraft unit.

The last English woman
tried for witchcraft
was convicted in 1944.

A quarter of
philosophers
believe in zombies.

Winston Churchill
was a druid.

Jimi Hendrix was a
paratrooper.

Madonna
was sacked from
Dunkin' Donuts for
squirting customers with jam.

Sylvester Stallone
was so broke before his
script for *Rocky* was accepted
that he sold his dog for $25.
A few weeks later, he bought it back
for $15,000.

Pavarotti holds the world record
for the most curtain calls:
he bowed 165 times
over the course
of an hour.

Regardless of household income,
children of authoritarian parents
are a third more likely to be obese.

1 in 3 children
can use a tablet
before they can speak.

Toddlers who
tell lies early on
are more likely to
do well later in life.

Humans
are born with a
sweet tooth.

80% of food
has sugar added
to it.

The caffeine
extracted from decaf coffee
is sold to soft-drinks
manufacturers.

Sugary drinks
kill 180,000 people
a year.

East African
vampire spiders
drink human blood
by eating mosquitoes
that have just bitten humans.

Every three seconds,
50 million cells in your body
die and are replaced.

A parking ticket
is issued in Britain
every four seconds.

The universe
is expanding
at 230 miles a second.

Clams can live
for more than
400 years.

An 80-year-old's fingernails
grow half as quickly
as a 30-year-old's.

Onychophagia
is the technical term
for biting your nails.

People with
a rare genetic disorder known as
'immigration delay disease'
have no fingerprints.

The expression
'the big C' as a
euphemism for cancer
was coined by John Wayne.

The first person
to smoke in Europe
was sent to prison for
being possessed by the devil.

Most people in the 18th century
only had a proper wash
twice a year.

In the 19th century,
circumcision was used to treat
epilepsy, hernia, lunacy
and paralysis.

Manchester United
Induced Addisonian Crisis
is a rare medical condition
involving heart palpitations
during Man United games.

1 in 4 people have
a hole in their heart.

The hole in the ozone layer
over Antarctica is
twice the size of Europe.

The hole in a guillotine
through which you stick your neck
is called a *lunette*.

The rules of golf
once provided that
if your ball hit your opponent,
he would lose the hole.

Celine Dion
owns a golf course.

Bill Murray
was once pulled over
by the Swedish police
for driving a golf cart
under the influence of alcohol.

In a 1776 version
of the rules of golf,
any ball falling in human excrement
could be removed for
a one-stroke penalty.

Golfers can get
'golf ball liver'
from licking their balls.

Alfred Lyttelton,
the first man to represent England
at both cricket and football,
was killed by a cricket ball.

William Hotten,
who wrote the first dictionary
of English slang in 1859,
died after eating too many
pork chops.

Human flesh
tastes like pork
but looks like beef.

37-stone Les Price was made to buy
two tickets for his flight from
Ireland to England, only to find that
the seats weren't in the same row.

Fat Man
was the name of
the bomb dropped on
Hiroshima.

You can burn 20% more fat
by exercising in the morning
on an empty stomach.

Taking the stairs
one step at a time
burns more calories than
taking them two at a time.

Having sex
uses the same number of
calories as there are
in one small
meringue.

Medieval peasants
ate twice as many calories
as we do today.

Medieval English
surnames included
Crakpot, Halfenaked, Swetinbedde
and Gyldenbollockes.

Viking names included
'desirous of beer', 'squat-wiggle',
'lust-hostage', 'short penis',
'able to fill a bay with fish by magic',
'the man who mixes his drinks' and
'the man without trousers'.

The Romans split France into
'Trousered Gaul' in the south
and 'Hairy Gaul' in the north.

Lewstery means
'to bustle about
like a lusty wench'.

Leint is an old
northern word meaning
'to add urine to ale
to make it stronger'.

Leep
is a Hindi word meaning
'to wash with water
and cow dung'.

Logodiarrhoea means
'talking too much'.

The human brain
has enough memory
to hold three million
hours of television.

Ross from *Friends*
celebrated his 29th birthday
in three consecutive seasons.

Matt LeBlanc
was down to his last $11
when he got the part of
Joey in *Friends*.

In most countries,
the most popular
programme on TV is
the weather forecast.

Not one of the *Star Trek*
TV shows or films
contains the words
'Beam me up, Scotty'.

The 1960s US TV show
Lost in Space
was set in 1997.

Fewer people
have ever been in space
than climbed Mount Everest
last year.

For every 25 people
who have reached the summit
of Mount Everest,
one person
has died trying.

47-year-old Mark Inglis
climbed Everest in 2006,
despite having no legs and
one of his prostheses snapping
in half at 21,000 feet.

'Viagra'
is a combination of
'virility' and 'Niagara'.

Tutankhamun
was the only ancient Egyptian
who was mummified with
an erect penis.

Tutankhamun's parents
were brother and sister.

(Q)

'Double cousins' share
all four grandparents.
This happens when
a pair of sisters marries
a pair of brothers.

One in five marriages
in the world are
between first cousins.

One in 20 couples argue
so much on their wedding night
they fail to consummate
their marriage.

George IV
got so drunk on his wedding night
he passed out on the floor
in front of the fireplace.

When Peter the Great
found out his wife had had an affair,
he had her lover's head chopped off
and presented to her in a jar.

In 2013,
Al-Qaeda apologised for
accidentally beheading
one of their own men.

More than twice as many people
were guillotined by the Nazis
as during the French Revolution.

The first violence
of the French Revolution
took place at a
luxury wallpaper factory.

Before having their chests cut open
and their hearts pulled out,
Aztec human-sacrifice victims
were given a cup of hot chocolate.

As well as humans,
the Aztecs sacrificed
wolves, turtles, snakes,
hummingbirds, woodpeckers
and shellfish.

In 2002, Norwegian footballer
Kenneth Kristensen signed for
third-division team Floey
and was paid his weight in shrimps.

Louis XIV ate 400 oysters
on his wedding night.

To improve their ability
to swallow hot dogs,
the International Federation of
Competitive Eating
is studying black holes.

Slum dwellings
made up 20% of the houses
in London in 1949.

It is illegal in Vancouver
to build a new house
with doorknobs.

Brass doorknobs
disinfect themselves
in a process known as
the oligodynamic effect.

Bacteria live for only three hours
on Croatia's currency, the kuna,
but for more than a day on the
Romanian leu.

It is as difficult
for a bacterium
to swim through water
as it is for a human
to swim through syrup.

The world's oceans
contain 20 million billion
tons of chlorine.

A chemical in ships' paint
causes female snails
to grow penises
and explode.

4% of the sand on
Normandy beaches
is made up of tiny metal particles
from the D-Day landings.

Half the world's population
has a genetic mutation that
makes Brussels sprouts
taste extremely nasty.

As a boy,
Roald Dahl taste-tested
new chocolate bars
for Cadbury's.

People who try to
stop thinking about chocolate
eat more of it than
those who don't.

1 in 5 British children
think fish fingers
are made of chicken.

1 in 5 kidneys
donated in the US
are thrown away because a
suitable recipient can't be found.

1 in 5 people in 2005
admitted to taking Derbisol
– a drug that doesn't exist.

Wamblecropt
is a 17th-century word
for 'indigestion'.

In Turkey,
the word for 'turkey' means
'Indian bird'.

The Indian word
for turkey means
'Peruvian bird'.

In Greece,
the word for 'turkey' means
'French bird'.

The Malaysian word
for 'turkey' means
'Dutch chicken'.

The world's largest
chicken nugget is
twice the size of the
world's largest chicken.

The world's largest water slide
in Kansas City
is taller than
Niagara Falls.

The dish of
the world's largest
single-aperture radio telescope is
large enough to hold the contents
of 357 million boxes of cornflakes.

The world's smallest advert
was stencilled onto
a bee's knee.

Piranha soup
is a popular aphrodisiac
in Brazil.

Prunes
were served as aphrodisiacs
in Elizabethan brothels.

Marmalade
was an aphrodisiac
in 17th-century London.

Frog juice,
made by putting
frogs in a blender,
is an aphrodisiac in Peru.

Before fridges were invented,
Russians and Finns
kept their milk fresh
by putting live frogs in it.

In 1998,
a swarm of jellyfish
in New Zealand
killed 56,000 salmon
in half an hour.

The national bird of Peru
is the Andean
cock of the rock.

The scientific name
for a llama
is *Lama glama*.

The first jerky
was called *charqui*
and was made from llama.

Male llamas having sex
make a strange gargling noise
called an 'orgle'.

The French word
for 'sexting'
is *textopornographique.*

The French for the
constellation Ursa Major is
'Le Casserole'.

The word *louche*
is French for
'cross-eyed'.

The French
for 'rehearsal'
is *répétition*.

In French episodes of
The Simpsons,
Homer's catchphrase 'D'oh!'
is dubbed as '*T'oh!*'

French names for trenches
in the First World War
included 'The Snail',
'Place de L'Opéra'
and 'Headache'.

Due to a computer error in 1989
41,000 Parisians received letters
charging them with murder,
extortion and prostitution
instead of traffic offences.

In 2013, a PayPal computer error
briefly made a man in Pennsylvania
the richest person in the world.

The richest man in Italy
is Michele Ferrero,
the maker of
Ferrero Rocher.

The most common occupation
for the wife of a millionaire
is teacher.

The first man to pass
the compulsory driving test
in Britain in 1935
was Mr Beene.

Thomas Edison
invented
the tattoo pen.

The man who invented the
water bed was unable to patent it
because it had already appeared
in science-fiction novels.

Titanic was the first movie
made by James Cameron that
didn't include any mention of
nuclear weapons.

Arnold Schwarzenegger earned
more than £20,000 per word
for his role in *Terminator 2*.

India's Mars probe cost less
than the movie *Gravity*.

The B-movie *The Blob*
is based on a real-life
police report
from 1950.

The movie *Blade Runner* was
based on a novel by Philip K. Dick.
Director Ridley Scott never
finished the book and Dick
never saw the film.

The last film
rented out by Blockbuster
was the 2013 comedy
This Is the End.

The Domesday Book
wasn't known as
the Domesday Book
for a hundred years
after it was written.

The Bible's
Book of Esther
doesn't mention God once.

There is no evidence
that Geoffrey Chaucer
ever visited Canterbury.

Not one of
the 500 references
to Geoffrey Chaucer
written in his lifetime
refers to him as a poet.

The first collection
of poetry published by
the three Brontë sisters
sold fewer copies
than it had authors.

Edgar Allan Poe
received only $9
for the publication of
The Raven.

Houdini
bought Edgar Allan Poe's
writing desk.

The novelist
Kurt Vonnegut
ran America's first
Saab dealership.

J. M. Barrie founded
a celebrity cricket team with
Arthur Conan Doyle, H. G. Wells,
Jerome K. Jerome, G. K. Chesterton,
A. A. Milne, Rudyard Kipling
and P. G. Wodehouse.

Cricket was allowed
under the Taliban,
but applause by the crowd
was banned.

Russell Brand's
My Booky Wook is banned
from Guantanamo Bay.

All glossy magazines
are radioactive.

Mouse sperm
is bigger than
elephant sperm.

The amniotic fluid
in the human womb
renews itself completely
every three hours.

The last entry in the
official Scrabble dictionary
is 'zzz'.

William Morton,
the father of anaesthesia,
first experimented on himself but
kept falling asleep before he could
describe the results.

To sleep for one night
in every bed in Las Vegas
would take 288 years.

The Bloody Mary has
been scientifically proven to be
the best alcoholic drink to
enjoy on an aeroplane.

Guglielmo Marconi,
the inventor of radio,
was the great-grandson
of the inventor of
Jameson's Irish whiskey.

It takes 700 grapes
to make one bottle of wine.

It takes a million
cloud droplets
to make one raindrop.

A planet called
HD 189733b,
63 light years from Earth,
is lashed by rain
made of molten glass
and 4,000 mph winds.

The word 'weather'
originally just meant
'wind'.

The Khasi Hills in India,
once known as the
wettest hills in the world,
are now having to import water.

Khaki
is Urdu for
'dust'.

Although Australia is
the driest inhabited continent,
Australians use more water
than anyone else.

The busiest polling station
in Australian elections
is in London.

Nobody won
the Nobel Peace Prize
in 1972.

J. R. R. Tolkien was rejected
for a Nobel Prize in Literature
on the grounds of his
'poor storytelling'.

Game of Thrones author
George R. R. Martin
adopted the 'R. R.' as
a homage to Tolkien.

In 2012,
146 girls in the US
were named Khaleesi.

In 2012,
five babies in the UK
were named Sherlock.

Chinese fans of *Sherlock* call
Benedict Cumberbatch
and Martin Freeman
'Curly Fu' and 'Peanut'.

The leader of
Brighton Council
is called Jason Kitcat.

The original KitKat
was an 18th-century
mutton pie.

Ruth Wakefield,
inventor of chocolate-chip cookies,
sold her idea to Nestlé in exchange
for a lifetime supply of chocolate.

Lava lamps
were invented by an accountant
whose hobby was making
underwater nudist films.

For inspiration,
D. H. Lawrence liked to climb
mulberry trees naked.

The world's oldest living tree
was already 100 years old
when Stonehenge
was built.

There's a tree
in South Africa so big that
a pub has been built
inside its trunk.

Palm trees
are a type of grass.

A grasshopper
becomes more sociable
if you stroke its hind legs.

Removing
a fruit fly's front legs
makes it bisexual.

Male fruit flies
given alcohol develop
homosexual tendencies.

Fruit flies
take their time
over difficult decisions.

After mating,
a pair of love bugs
can stay stuck together,
even in flight,
for several days.

Male woodlice
can change sex
but females can't.

Every leech
has 18 testicles
and two ovaries.

The largest-ever leech
was 18 inches long and
went by the name of
Grandma Moses.

There is a species of leech
that can survive 24 hours
in liquid nitrogen.

A leech can
take up to 200 days
to digest
a meal.

'Email'
is a 16th-century word
meaning 'enamel'.

The Dutch Crown jewels
are made of fake pearls,
fish scales and
coloured foil.

The Pantone colour chart
has 104 shades of grey.

Fifty Shades of Grey
was originally titled
Masters of the Universe.

The first baseball gloves
were flesh-coloured in case
spectators noticed and accused
players of cowardice.

According to England's
leading brain surgeon,
it is more dangerous
to wear a cycle helmet
than not to wear one.

St George
is the patron saint of
England, leprosy and syphilis.

The largest sperm bank in the world
does not accept donations
from redheads because of
'insufficient demand'.

Dormice
are not mice.

Fish
can yawn.

Elephants
tickle each other.

The technical term for
guffawing is
gargalesis.

The Norwegian word
for smelly feet is *tåfis*,
which means 'toe-fart'.

Conversesjukan is Swedish for
foot problems caused by
wearing trendy trainers.

It is illegal
to wear a bikini in Barcelona,
except on the beach.

Miniskirts
are illegal in Uganda.

Q

It is illegal
to take mineral water
into Nigeria.

NEPA,
the former Nigerian
electric power authority,
was popularly known as
'Never Electric Power Anytime'.

From 1934 to 1948,
the motto of the BBC was
Quaecunque, Latin for
'Whatever'.

The original
BBC licence fee
cost the equivalent of
50p.

The price the
tooth fairy pays for a tooth
went up by 42% between
2011 and 2013.

Queen Victoria
had jewellery made out of
her children's milk teeth.

The Romans used
powdered mouse brains
as toothpaste.

At the 2012 London Olympics,
55% of the athletes were found
to have tooth decay.

Lipstick in the US
may legally contain lead,
arsenic and mercury.

At the court of Louis XIV
women used lemons
to redden their lips.

The Romans
used lemons as
mothballs.

Casanova
used half a lemon
as an improvised
contraceptive.

At 21,
Mussolini was
homeless and living under
a bridge in Switzerland.

Waterloo Bridge is
called the Ladies Bridge
because it was built
mainly by women.

Kissing was
banned in England
in 1439.

It takes five people
to extract semen
from a vulture.

In 1859,
a moral panic swept America
over young people playing
too much chess.

In 1937,
ukuleles were banned in Japan
on the grounds that they
'weakened young people's will'.

In 1816,
The Times warned its readers
that the waltz was
'a fatal contagion'.

In 1916,
New Jersey banned the Charleston
because it was thought to cause
broken shins.

More than a third
of all sick leave
is taken on Mondays.

Vaccinations
don't work
on octopuses.

Hermit crabs
form gangs
to steal shells from
other hermit crabs.

The average haul per robber
for a bank raid is
£12,706.60.

If you earn
£20,250 a year,
you're one of the
world's richest 1%.

In 2000,
it cost $3 billion to
sequence a human genome.
By 2014, the cost had fallen
to under $1,000.

In 1981,
there were 2,420
Britons over the age of 100.
By 2012, there were
12,320.

By 2050,
70% of people
will live in cities.

Birds living in cities
start the dawn chorus
five hours earlier than
in the countryside.

Alligators balance
twigs on their noses,
to lure birds looking for
nest-building materials.

Dogs with
ADHD make
the best sniffer dogs.

Only one dog
was ever registered as
a Japanese prisoner of war.

During the First World War,
German and Russian troops agreed
a ceasefire and joined forces to
fend off attacks by wolves.

To make them less conspicuous,
white horses in the British army
in the First World War were
dyed brown with food colouring.

Aristotle advised
Alexander the Great
not to let his soldiers drink mint tea
because it would make them
think more of love than war.

In the Hundred Years War,
dead soldiers had their
faces burned off with hot irons
to prevent identification.

Q

London burnt down in 1077, 1087,
1132, 1136, 1203, 1212, 1220
and 1227, as well as 1666.

A search for 'singular coincidence'
in the British Newspaper Archive
brings up more than 10,000 articles.

On 17 April 2011,
Emmanuel Mutai
won the London Marathon.
The next day, Geoffrey Mutai
won the Boston Marathon.
The two men are not related.

In April 1971,
the headmaster of
a Japanese primary school
found a new species of salamander
in the school drains.

Bacteria
remain
eternally young.

In 1899,
Dr Horace Emmett revealed
that the secret of eternal youth
was injections of ground-up
squirrel testicles.
He died later that year.

The world's shortest snake
is four inches long
and often mistaken
for an earthworm.

The curly part
of a corkscrew
is called the 'worm'.

Q

Kiwi fruit
used to be called
'melonettes'.

Humans are not at
the top of the food chain
but near the middle,
on a level with pigs
and anchovies.

Dorothy Parker
had a pet canary
she called Onan
because he spilled his
seed on the ground.

Salvador Dalí
had a pet anteater.

Giant anteaters
eat 30,000 ants a day.

There are
1.6 million people
in Manhattan
and 1.2 billion ants.

The total amount of adrenaline
in half a million people
weighs ⅟30th of an ounce.

The richest 85 people in the world
have as much money as
the poorest 3.5 billion.

Sir Francis Drake
left all his money to the
poor people of Plymouth.

When Handel died,
he left the equivalent of £86,000
to build a monument to himself
in Westminster Abbey.

The amount of money you get
at the start of Monopoly (£1,500)
is the current average weekly rent
in central London.

In London SW3,
£100 would buy you
a piece of property
the size of an
Oyster card.

One in 11 people on Earth
earn their money
from tourism.

The Great Wall of China
was funded by a state lottery.

The lottery of the
Zimbabwe Banking Corporation
was won in 2000 by the
president of Zimbabwe.

President Mugabe has
been in power 50% longer
than the lifetime of
the average Zimbabwean.

Saddam Hussein's regime
destroyed 90% of
Iraq's marshes.

Members of the
Yazidi religion of Iraq
are forbidden to
eat lettuce.

Varieties of lettuce include:
Amish Deer Tongue,
Drunken Woman,
Midnight Ruffles and
Red Leprechaun.

Nero
ate leeks
to improve his
singing voice.

Edward II
employed a 'tumbler'
who fell off his horse
to amuse the king for
20 shillings a time.

King Francis I of France
hung the *Mona Lisa*
in his bathroom.

Queen Elizabeth II had a
special shelf installed in her car
so there was somewhere
to put her handbag.

King Olav V of Norway
preferred to travel
by public transport.

John Lennon and George Harrison
once got a bus across Liverpool
to visit a man who could
teach them the
chord B7.

Liverpudlians
buy three times as
many false eyelashes
as the national average.

In the 18th century,
people with facial scars
filled them in with lard
and painted them over
with white lead.

Two teaspoonfuls of Botox
are enough to kill
everyone in Britain.

A 'quarter pounder'
weighs less than
a fifth of a pound
when cooked.

Mrs Beeton
recommended
boiling pasta
for 1¾ hours.

Cornish pasties
make more money each year
than Tonga, Micronesia
or the Cook Islands.

Shemomedjamo
is a Georgian word meaning
'to eat past the point of fullness
because the food is so delicious'.

In Georgian,
mama means 'father'
and *deda* means 'mother'.

The Inuit word *iktsuarpok*
means 'to keep going outside
to see if anyone's coming'.

The Japanese word *tsundoku*
means buying books
and not getting around
to reading them.

*Gurkentrupp*e
is German for 'losers':
literally, an
'army of cucumbers'.

The world's first nudist colony,
founded in India in 1891, was called
the Fellowship of the Naked Trust.

The expression 'flash mob'
was first used in 1832 and meant
a group of petty criminals.

Libya was the first country to
issue an arrest warrant
for Osama bin Laden.

The first ever webcam
was in the computer lab
at Cambridge University.
It was trained on the
coffee pot in the corridor
to save the scientists
making pointless trips
when it had run out.

Coffee beans
are actually seeds.

Sunflower seeds
are actually fruits.

Fruits
are the ovaries
of plants.

In order to be
light enough to fly,
birds have
only one ovary.

Men with smaller testicles
tend to be better fathers.

Ramajit Raghav became
the world's oldest father
at 96 years old.

At least 10%
of all the adult cheetahs
in the southern Serengeti
have the same mother.

A male cheetah
can make a female ovulate
by barking at her.

An elephant call
can be heard anywhere
within 100 square miles.

Elephants can tell different
human languages apart.

Elephants have
more muscles in their trunks
than adult humans have
in their entire body.

Over 80 international brands
feature the word 'Maasai'.
Collectively worth billions,
none has sought permission
from the Maasai people.

Nike's 'Just Do It' slogan
was inspired by
the last words
of a murderer.

Six streets in London
had their names changed
after murders took place there.

The villains in *Psycho*,
The Texas Chainsaw Massacre
and *The Silence of the Lambs*
are all based on the same man.

In 2002, an American bomber
attempted to plant 18 bombs
which, when they exploded,
would form a giant smiley face.

In 1552,
Henry Pert died after
shooting himself in the face
with his own bow and arrow.

Head lice
will die if they don't
eat six times a day.

Theodore Roosevelt
thought it was a shame
diplodocuses had died out:
he'd have liked to hunt one.

When a pope dies,
his seals are defaced and
his ring is split in two.

Sigmund Freud
treated Gustav Mahler
for impotence.

A popular way to cure impotence
in the 14th century
was to wear your trousers
on your head for 24 hours.

The Duke of Wellington
was kicked out of his club in 1814
for wearing trousers
instead of pantaloons.

'Extraordinary affair,'
said the Duke of Wellington
after his first Cabinet meeting.
'I gave them their orders and they
wanted to stay to discuss them . . .'

The Duke of Wellington's horse,
Copenhagen, died from eating
too many sponge cakes, bath buns
and chocolate creams.

Przewalski's horses,
a rare, wild breed
native to Mongolia,
have never been domesticated.

The two pandas
in Edinburgh Zoo
eat £40,000 worth
of food a year.

Pandas defecate
50 times a day.

In Bolivia,
llama droppings are
used to purify water.

Polluted water
kills children at a rate
equivalent to a fully laden
jumbo jet crashing
every four hours.

Since 1948,
100 planes have
gone missing in flight
and never been recovered.

In the UK,
one child goes missing
every five minutes.

It's impossible to
get lost in a labyrinth:
unlike mazes, labyrinths have
only one possible route.

Fearing a German invasion,
in 1940 Alan Turing converted
his assets into silver ingots and
buried them in Buckinghamshire.
He spent the rest of his life
failing to find them.

80%
of all time capsules
have been lost.

11,000 keys are lost
on London's Tubes
and buses every year.

The Tube ride between
Leicester Square and Covent Garden
is 260 metres long, costs £4.30,
and is the most popular journey
among tourists.

Until 1900,
visitors to Stonehenge
were given chisels so they could
chip off a souvenir.

Gift
is German for
'poison'.

Gift cards
worth £240 million
go unredeemed in
Britain each year.

Ⓠ

The Queen's staff
get to choose their own
Christmas presents, which
must be worth between
£20 and £25.

The Queen
took her corgi, Susan,
on her honeymoon.

1 in 4 American dogs
are overweight.

People who kiss their dogs
have lower blood pressure
than those who don't.

1 in 5 people in Wales
haven't been kissed
for a year.

People who
believe in luck
are luckier than
those who don't.

The chances
of finding a
four-leaf clover
are 10,000–1.

The most leaves
ever found on
a clover
is 12.

Frank Sinatra
took a shower
12 times a day.

Months that
begin on a Sunday
will always have a
Friday the 13th.

Stan Laurel was
originally called Stan Jefferson.
He changed his name because
it had 13 letters in it.

Stan Laurel once
successfully cross-bred
a potato with an onion,
but couldn't persuade
anyone to eat one.

The racehorse
Potooooooooo
got its name from
a stable-hand who
couldn't spell
'Potato'.

One-third of
British potatoes
are made into chips.

Two-thirds of the
bagged salad sold by Tesco
never gets eaten.

Nicknames for stinging nettles
include 'the devil's leaf'
and 'naughty man's plaything'.

The *Forme of Cury,*
a 14th-century English cookbook,
has a recipe for
porpoise haggis.

Archibald Clark West,
the inventor of Doritos,
had them sprinkled
on his grave.

Plywood
was invented by
Alfred Nobel's father

Abraham Lincoln's wife
was an opium addict.

Dmitri Mendeleev
was working as a
cheese consultant
when he had the idea
for the periodic table.

In 2013,
nine babies born in the UK
were named
Cheese.

Lady cheese
is cheese made from
human breast milk.

Cannibalism
in the UK
is legal.

A 12½-stone man
contains
110,000 calories.

People eat less
in subdued lighting.

The record number
of live goldfish swallowed
at a single sitting
is 210.

The seventh
most common sentence
in *The Hunger Games* trilogy is
'I swallowed hard.'

The fastest swallow in nature
is that of the frogfish,
which sucks its prey down
in 0.006 seconds.

The International Space Station
travels at five miles a second.

A day on the
International Space Station
is 1½ hours long.

The universe
is getting less blue
and more red.

Martian sunsets
are blue.

When humans
first evolved on Earth,
there was water on Mars.

Craters on Mars
under 60 kilometres in diameter
are named after towns on Earth
with populations under 100,000.

The first choice of a name for
Disney's Hannah Montana
was Alexis Texas, but it
was already taken
by a porn star.

Before he started eating cookies,
the Cookie Monster's name
was Sid.

The name Chewbacca
is from *saboka*,
the Russian for 'dog'.

Chewbacca's voice
was created by combining
the sounds of a bear, a walrus,
a lion and a badger.

Disney was sued
by a biologist for
defaming the character of hyenas
in *The Lion King*.

The mayor of the city
of Batman in Turkey
threatened to sue Warner Bros
for not asking permission to use
the city's name in the *Batman* movies.

To kit yourself out
as a real-life Batman
would cost about
$300 million.

Christian Bale's
father's uncle's cousin
was the Edwardian actress
Lily Langtry.

Clark Kent is two inches
shorter than Superman;
to finesse his secret identity
he compresses his spine.

When the infant Mozart
first rose to prominence,
some members of the Royal Society
thought he was a dwarf in disguise.

Mozart's sister
was also a musician,
who sometimes took top billing
as they toured Europe together.

As a child,
Mozart was terrified
of trumpets.

An ear trumpet
is technically known as
an *otacousticon*.

A *wheeple*
is an ineffectual attempt
to whistle loudly.

An ass-pipe
is a musical instrument
from the British Virgin Islands,
made from a car exhaust
and played like a tuba.

The *izikhothane*
are a South African gang
who meet in car parks,
cover themselves in custard
and burn wads of cash.

'Bitch the pot'
was 19th-century slang for
'pour the tea'.

Perfect coffee
should consist of
17.42 units of water
for every unit of coffee.

Swedes
drink twice as much coffee
as Americans.

In 1820, the average American
drank half a pint of whisky
every day.

The longer a whisky is aged,
the longer it takes for your body
to get rid of the alcohol.

The average Belarusian
drinks 17.5 litres
of alcohol a year.

Belarus has the
same infant-mortality rate
as Birmingham.

Chemicals caused
female munitions workers
in the First World War to
give birth to yellow babies.

Bananas
have more trade
regulations
than AK-47s.

There are more species of plant
on Cape Town's Table Mountain
than in the whole of the UK.

Five times as many
Cadbury's Creme Eggs
are eaten in Britain every year
as there are people.

A kiwi's egg is
so large it's equivalent to
a human mother giving birth
to a six-year-old.

Dr Seuss wrote
Green Eggs and Ham
to win a bet with his publisher
that he couldn't write a book
using just 50 different words.

The French phrase *au gratin*
literally means
'with scrapings'.

There are no mentions
of salad in the Bible.

**You are more likely
to believe a statement
that is printed in bold.**

Taking a photo of something
reduces your ability
to remember it.

90% of people
remember their first kiss
more vividly than
the first time they had sex.

A woman who is
bitten by a cat has
a 50% chance of
being diagnosed
with depression.

Chessington
World of Adventures has
banned animal-print onesies
to stop the animals there
getting confused.

More than 60% of
pandas born in captivity
die within a week.

The UK
turtle-dove population
has declined by 95%
since 2005.

In 2013,
160 sheep were stolen
from the Dorset village
of Wool.

In 1557,
Robert Calf
was mauled to death
by a cow.

Tupperware
was invented by a
chicken salesman.

Colonel Sanders's
career as a lawyer came to an end
when he assaulted his
client in court.

There is a law firm
in Leeds called
Godloves Solicitors.

The real name of
the rapper Aloe Blacc is
Egbert Nathaniel Dawkins III.

'Yahoo'
is an acronym for
'Yet
Another
Hierarchical
Officious
Oracle'.

Yoda's
first name
is Minch.

Woody from *Toy Story*'s
last name is
Pride.

Matt Groening's mother
was called Marge Wiggum.

The 2003 world poker champion
who won $2.5 million
for a $39 entry fee
is called Chris Moneymaker.

In 1910,
a man called Morton Norbury
was killed after an argument
over who had the most
handsome moustache.

In the 19th century,
pious Spaniards grew moustaches
in the shape of a cross.

Abraham Lincoln
only had a beard for
the last five years of his life.

Charles Darwin
only grew his famous beard
in his mid-fifties to
relieve his eczema.

Beard trimming
is banned by the Bible.

The prophet Muhammad
dyed his beard
with henna.

The Paris Exhibition of 1855
had a life-sized picture
of Queen Victoria
made of hair.

John Constable
was 39 when he sold
his first landscape painting.

Picasso
painted using
ordinary house paint.

The US army
keeps Hitler's watercolours in
a high-security warehouse
in Virginia.

Until the 1960s,
there was a paint
called 'Mummy Brown'.
They stopped making it
when the manufacturers
ran out of mummies.

The ancient Egyptians
mummified beef ribs,
sliced duck and goat meat
to eat in the afterlife.

The Great Pyramid of Giza
was built by 100,000 people
working 10 hours a day
for 20 years.

The ancient Egyptians
invented the will
and the business handshake.

Ancient Egyptian lettuce
contained the same
active ingredient
as cocaine.

Old English medicines included
'Allan's Nipple Liniment',
'Grimston's Eye Snuff',
'Miller's Worm Plums' and
'Italian Bosom Friend'.

People suffering from
superior canal dehiscence syndrome
can hear their own eyeballs moving.

An 'eye-baby'
is the tiny reflection of yourself
in someone else's eye.

Reflectors on
pedestrians' clothing are
a legal requirement in Estonia.

It is against the law
for anyone in Barbados
to wear camouflage.

Until January 2013,
it was illegal for
women in Paris
to wear trousers.

Women called Eleanor
are 100 times more likely
to get into Oxford University
than women called Jade.

'Chopsticks'
was written by
a 16-year-old girl.

More than a million square feet
of forest are used every year
to make chopsticks.

It is cheaper
to send Scottish cod to China
to be filleted and sent back again
than to fillet the fish
in Scotland.

If you feed fish
prawn-cocktail Skips,
they turn pink.

Only six out of 22
crocodile species present
any danger to humans.

When Barack Obama visited
Australia's Northern Territory,
he was given a $50,000
crocodile-attack insurance policy.

People
will gamble more
if they are holding a crocodile.

Male chess players
adopt riskier strategies when
playing against beautiful women.

Only 2,000 women
in the world buy
haute-couture dresses.
It takes 2,200
seamstresses
to make them.

In 13th-century France,
it was illegal to sew
more than 50 silver buttons
onto your clothes.

The Scottish Official Board
of Highland Dancing
says that under their kilts
Scotsmen should wear
dark underpants.

In 1320, Scotland
was excommunicated
by the Pope.

There are eight million
Jehovah's Witnesses on Earth
but, according to their teachings,
only 144,000 people will be
saved at the end of the world.

Lloyd's of London
once offered reduced premiums
for missionary ships because
they had divine protection.

In 2005,
a Romanian murderer sued God
for not doing enough to
protect him from Satan.

The world's best-selling
genre of literature
is self-help books.

The most common sentence
in the *Harry Potter* books is
'Nothing happened.'

The most common
starting price of
Grand National winners
is 25/1.

The most commonly
awarded grade
at Harvard
is an A.

The most commonly asked question
at Hanna-Barbera's head office is:
'What did Barney Rubble
do for a living?'

The first-ever comic strip
was published at the suggestion of
Wolfgang von Goethe.

The original Popeye
got his strength from
rubbing a magic hen.

The DC Comics character
Snowflame
got his superpowers
from cocaine.

Until 1916,
cocaine and heroin
could be bought
over the counter
at Harrods.

Crisp packets
aren't full of air;
they're full of nitrogen.

Hula Hoops
are not kosher.

Orthodox Jews
can buy kosher
sexual lubricants.

The Hebrew
for 'usury' is
ribbit.

Male Darwin frogs
store their tadpoles
in their vocal sacs,
then cough up
fully formed frogs.

There is a drug
made from the saliva
of the Gila monster that
stops you feeling hungry.

Anole lizards
do press-ups
to get attention.

If you fire lasers
at the brain of a fly,
you can make it have sex
with a ball of wax.

2014 was
the International Year of
the Salamander,
the Family, the Secretary,
and the Spine.

In its first year,
the human brain
grows to 75%
of its full size.

Blackbeard
was a pirate
for two years.

Snails
can sleep for
three years.

The British army's
Cyclist Corps
lasted four years.

Five baby girls
in the US in 2012
were named
Cricket.

Baby chickens
use their right eye
to look for food
and their left eye
to look out for predators.

A baby porcupine
is called a porcupette.

The genome of wheat
is five times larger
than the human genome.

Before the
invention of electricity,
human beings slept for
90 minutes longer
than they do now.

Elizabeth I
always slept with
another woman in her bed.

Elizabeth I
owned 3,000 dresses
and the world's first
wire coat hanger.

Elizabeth I
invented
gingerbread men.

Robert Louis Stevenson
dreamt the plot of
Dr Jekyll and Mr Hyde.

Joseph Conrad
died leaving an
unfinished novel
called *Suspense*.

It took 17 takes
for E. B. White to
record the death scene for the
audiobook of *Charlotte's Web*
without breaking down.

Hugh Hefner
has someone preselect
his potato chips so he
doesn't have to eat
broken ones.

Franz Kafka
liked to exercise naked
in front of the window.

Humans
are the only animals
that blush.

Snakes
don't have eyelids.

Whales
get tan lines.

Ants
don't have ears.

All the ants in the world
weigh about the same
as all the people.

There are more stars
in the universe
than words have been spoken
by all of the humans
who have ever lived.

It would take
225 million years
to walk a light year.

Swinging your arms
when walking
makes it 12% easier.

Ⓠ

70% of all train journeys
in England start or finish
in London.

The London Underground
was originally intended
to terminate in Paris.

In 2014,
a single parking space
in London was sold
for £400,000.

Spitalfields
in London
used to be known as
Lolsworth.

Archers Way
in Doncaster
was formerly called
Butt Hole Road.

The first T-shirt
was aimed at bachelors
who couldn't sew on buttons.

Charles Darwin's
cousin Francis Galton
invented underwater spectacles
so he could read in the bath.

After getting out of the bath,
the ancient Greeks
covered themselves
with olive oil.

If everyone washed
their hands properly with soap,
it would save 600,000
lives a year.

Every year,
around 3,000 people
get bubonic plague.

Medical mistakes kill
enough Americans each week
to fill four 747s.

13 Americans
have died as a result of
laxative overdose.

If the US national debt were
stacked in $5 bills, it would reach
three-quarters of the way
to the Moon.

If Bill Gates gave his entire fortune
to the US government, it would
only cover the national deficit
for 15 days.

If you have no debts
and £10 in your pocket,
you are wealthier than
a quarter of Americans.

The Pentagon
is successfully hacked
250,000 times a year,
and unsuccessfully hacked
10 million times a day.

28% of Americans
believe a secret elite is
conspiring to run the world.

70% of the silent movies
made in America
have been lost.

The cross-eyed
silent-film comedian
Ben Turpin
had his eyes insured
against uncrossing.

None of an octopus's limbs
knows what any of the
others are doing.

The Lord of the Rings
holds the record for the
greatest number of false feet
used in a single movie:
60,000.

The cast of
Riverdance
have worn out
14,000 pairs of shoes.

The V&A Museum
has a 1,500-year-old pair of socks
designed to be worn with sandals.

The world's first GPS shoes
are activated by clicking
the heels three times.

Shoes with
five eyelets on each side
can be laced up
51,840 different ways.

There are
177,147
ways to tie a tie.

In imperial Japan,
high-born women
peed standing-up
so as not to crease
their kimonos.

Louis XIV
announced his engagement
from the lavatory.

At Stalin's funeral
500 people were
trampled to death.

Of the 142 million deaths
caused by an ideology
in the 20th century
94 million were due
to communism.

Lenin
owned nine Rolls-Royces.

According to the International
Trade Union Confederation,
British workers have
fewer rights than
Albanians, Russians
or Rwandans.

The chairman of a company
is four times more likely
to be a psychopath
than the doorman.

Members of the Mafia
are much less likely
to be psychopaths than
other Italian criminals.

Prison inmates in Chile
have better mental health
than the average American.

There are more libraries
in Britain's prisons
than there are in its schools.

Keeping a criminal in prison
costs £42,000 a year,
£8,730 more than the
annual school fees
at Eton.

The annual cost to the UK economy
of reoffending by ex-prisoners
is equivalent to staging
the Olympics
every year.

In 19th-century Britain,
prisoners were let out for the day
if they paid a fee of £5
(equivalent to £300 today).

Australia's first police force
was composed of the
best-behaved convicts.

Before 1902,
it was illegal for Australians
to swim at the beach
during the day.

In 1907,
Australian dancer Victor Goulet
had one of his Achilles tendons
replaced with a wallaby's.

Crop circles in Australia
are caused by frenzied wallabies
who get high in the poppy fields
used to grow legal opium.

A *peppier* is a waiter
whose sole job is
to go round with a
pepper grinder.

78% of
Bulgarians
never do any exercise.

The average
Internet user
goes online
34 times a day.

A group of hackers
once took down
Papa John's website
because their pizza was late.

90% of Britons
eat pizza
at least once a week.

24% of Britons
eat cereal for supper
at least once a week.

Until the 1940s,
fake snow in the movies
was made by painting
cornflakes white.

It's a Wonderful Life
won just one Oscar:
for Technical Achievement
in developing a new kind
of artificial snow.

Frank Capra
had a lucky raven called Jimmy
who appeared in all his movies
between 1938 and 1946.

The lapwing has more names than
any other British bird, including:
Pie-wipe, Chewit, Toppyup,
Peasiewheep, Tee-ick, Tee-ack,
Tee-o, Teewhup, Ticks Nicket,
Tieve's Nacket, Wallock, Wallop,
Wallopie Wep, Horneywink,
Horny Wick and Hornpie.

'At sparrowsfart'
is slang for
'very early in the morning'.

The Anna's hummingbird
chirps with its bottom.

The scientific name
for the milk thistle
is *Silybum*.

There is a genus of
tiny sea snails called *Bittium*,
and a genus of even tinier ones
called *Ittibittium*.

The *Gelae* genus
of slime mould beetles includes
Gelae baen, *Gelae belae*,
Gelae donut, *Gelae fish*
and *Gelae rol*.

There are chemicals called
arsole, urantae, fucol,
dogcollarane, apatite
and cummingtonite.

The largest molecule in nature
is chromosome 1.
All human beings have two of them,
and each contains 10 billion atoms.

Half of all human beings
have mites living
in their eyelashes.

The California mite
Paratarsotomus macropalpis
can run 300 of its own
body lengths per second:
20 times faster than a cheetah.

A cheetah
can go from 0 to 40 mph
in three strides.

Lions
can get hairballs
the size of footballs.

385 million years ago,
fish had fingers.

Four million years ago,
rats in South America
were the size of hippos.

The world's oldest rose bush
is 1,000 years old.

Apples, strawberries,
plums and almonds
are all types of rose.

A whole orange
will float on water,
but sinks if you peel it.

All tardigrades
live in water
but none of them
can swim.

Because the Pacific island
of Guam has no sand,
all the roads are
made of coral.

Coral reefs
make up only 1%
of the ocean floor,
but are home to 25%
of all ocean life.

95% of the
underwater world
is yet to be explored.

If Mount Everest
stood on the bottom
of the Marianas Trench,
there would be over a mile
of water between its summit
and the surface of the sea.

Emperor penguins
can dive deeper
than the height of the
Empire State Building.

There is more water
in the Earth's core
than in all of its oceans.

If the Earth
had no clouds,
the sea would
evaporate.

The floods in Australia
in 2010 and 2011 caused
the world's sea levels to drop
by seven millimetres.

If you removed the water
from every life form on Earth,
it would be enough to
cover the Isle of Man
to a depth of half a mile.

In the California gold rush,
water cost more than gold.

If you hold your breath
and put your face in cold water,
your heart will immediately
slow down by 25%.

Squirting cold water
into your left ear
will make you feel
less optimistic.

You Only Live Once
is Katie Price's fourth
autobiography.

40% of humanity
live in countries where
it's illegal to be
homosexual.

The age boys reach puberty has
dropped by 2½ months
every decade since
the mid-1700s.

A bite from a Russell's pit viper
can send the victim
back through puberty.

Frogs find their way back
to their breeding grounds
by following the smell
of the pond's algae.

Photographs of Algae,
published in 1845,
was the first book
ever to contain
photographs.

Charles Darwin's
last book was called
*The Formation of Vegetable Mould
through the Action of Worms.*

1 in 10 Icelanders
will publish a book
at some time in their life.

It's illegal in Iceland
for parents to threaten children
with fictional characters.

In the French
Harry Potter books,
Voldemort's middle name
is Elvis.

Elvis
was naturally blond.

Blond footballers
are 15% more likely
to score in penalty shootouts
than dark-haired ones.

Dolly Parton
once lost a Dolly Parton
lookalike competition
to a drag artist.

A leading comedian in Iran
was banned from acting
for eight years because
he looked too much
like the president.

The president of North Korea
is Kim Il-sung, who
died in 1994.

Kim Jong-un,
Supreme Leader of North Korea,
is the world's youngest
head of state.

The film of
Gone with the Wind
is banned in North Korea,
but virtually every adult there
has read the book.

'Gangnam Style' has been watched
for four times more hours than
it took to build the Great Pyramid.

Queen
Cleopatra
lived closer
in time to the
Moon landings
than to the building
of the Great Pyramid.

The world's oldest building
is a Japanese hut built
half a million years before
the Great Pyramid.

'Meh'
is the sound that
Japanese sheep make.

Sheep can
see behind themselves
without moving their heads.

Human beings
had been keeping
sheep for 7,000 years
before it occurred to anyone
to use their wool.

One-third
of takeaway lamb curries
contain meat
other than lamb.

The average Briton
passes 32 takeaways
between home and work.

More people in the world
recognise the McDonald's symbol
than the Christian cross.

When the first McDonald's
drive-through in Kuwait opened,
the queue was seven miles long.

Usain Bolt
ate 1,000 chicken nuggets
during the Beijing Olympics
because he didn't like
Chinese food.

Velociraptors
were the size of
large chickens.

On average Britons will eat
1,126 chickens
in their lifetime.

(i)

During its lifetime,
the International Space Station
will be hit by 100,000 meteoroids.

There are 1,397
known asteroids capable of
causing 'major devastation'
if they hit the Earth.

The theoretical process of
knocking a meteoroid off course
with a nuclear explosion
is called an 'X-ray slap'.

In 1958, the US Air Force
planned to detonate
a nuclear bomb on the Moon to
demonstrate US military supremacy.

(i)

In 1971, 100 copies
of the Bible were
taken to the Moon.

The Moon has earthquakes
that last for up to 10 minutes.
Because it's so dry and dense,
they make it vibrate
like a tuning fork.

The dark side of the Moon
is turquoise.

In China,
the Man in the Moon
is known as
the Toad in the Moon.

One-third of toads
crossing roads
are fatally run over.

Polar bears
cannot be seen by using
night-vision
equipment.

Tortoises
can feel it
if you touch
their shells.

Only 1 in 1,000
leatherback turtles
survive to adulthood.

In 1860,
girls in the West
reached puberty at 16½.
Now they get there
before they're 10.

According to Catholic tradition,
the 'Limbo of the Children'
is a nursery on the edge of Hell
for unbaptised infants.

70% of Americans
believe in the existence
of the devil.

Finnair
operates a daily flight
666 to HEL.

Neil Armstrong's
spacesuit
was made by a
bra manufacturer.

Neil Armstrong's
boots are still
floating around
in space.

Humans spend
13% of their lives
not focusing on
anything in
particular.

44% of women prefer
reading *Fifty Shades of Grey*
to actually having sex.

Male ladybirds can spend
up to four hours mating with a
dead female before realising
something is wrong.

Ladybird orgasms
last for 30 minutes.

Smaller
animals
experience
time as
passing
more
slowly.

'*Time* Person of the Year'
contains the first, second and third
most commonly used nouns
in English, in order.

Lancaster County, Pennsylvania,
has towns called
Intercourse and Paradise.
It takes six minutes to get from
one to the other.

Michigan has towns called
Paradise and Hell
that are less than
300 miles apart.

The world's most expensive
phone number is 666-6666.
It was sold in 2006
for £1.5 million.

1 in 6 mobile phones
in Britain are contaminated
with faecal matter.

The most common bacteria
found on banknotes are
the ones that cause acne.

There are more than
£100 million worth of 1p coins
in circulation in the UK.

Borrowing £400 from Wonga
at its standard rate for seven years
would leave you owing more than
Britain's national debt.

In the UK in 2013,
more than 4,000 people
were buried in paupers' graves.

Hospital,
a village in Ireland,
doesn't have
a hospital.

The IKEA store
on Calle Me Falta un Tornillo
('I've Got a Screw Loose Street')
in Valladolid, Spain, is hard to find
because people keep stealing
the street signs.

Spanish police are called smurfs
because they wear pale-blue hats.

Tipping the hat
comes from the military salute,
which in turn comes from
men in armour lifting the visor
to show their faces.

The long black ribbon
round a funeral director's
top hat is called
a weeper.

The Queen Mother
once turned up unannounced
to watch a top-secret rehearsal
of her own funeral.

The ashes of
one in 50 people
who are cremated
are never collected
by relatives.

Cremation causes
silicone breast implants
to explode.

A Spartan only got
his name on his tombstone
if he died in battle.

Vikings who died in bed
rather than in battle
went to a special afterlife
where it was always foggy.

The oldest person in history
smoked for 96 years.

One-third of babies
born in Britain in 2013
are expected to live
for a century.

Emperor Hirohito's
final speech to the Japanese nation
was the first time his subjects
had ever heard his voice.

Einstein's last words
were spoken in German to a
nurse who didn't speak German
and are lost for ever.

Bing Crosby's
last words were:
'That was a great
game of golf, fellers.'

The last words
of John Le Mesurier were:
'It's all been rather lovely.'

Don't Believe a Word of It?

To check any fact, go to qi.com/1411 and type the relevant page number into the search box. Click on the online sources for a wide range of background material.

Acknowledgements

The heart and soul of QI is the happy band of brilliant researchers known as the QI Elves. For this book, Anne Miller, Andrew Hunter Murray, Anna Ptaszynski and Alex Bell did most of the serious digging, with the help of the rest of our pointy-eared team: Mandy Fenton, Piers Fletcher, Molly Oldfield and Justin Pollard, with Rob Blake, Will Bowen, Jack Burke, Jenny Doughty, Chris Gray, Freddy Soames and Liz Townsend. We're also grateful for some excellent last-minute material from two non-Elves, Jane Hancock and Sam Cable.

Q

The book was masterminded by our beloved editor, Sarah Lloyd, with the expert help of Ian Bahrami and Jill Burrows, and published by our friends at Faber & Faber, Britain's best Book Gnomes, headed by Stephen Page, Julian Loose, Eleanor Crow, Anne Owen, John Grindrod, Sophie Portas and Hannah Griffiths.

Email us at Elves@qi.com if you have a query, quibble or correction. Stay in touch with us on facebook.com/OfficialQI, at @qikipedia on Twitter, or by visiting qi.com, which is different every day. You might also like the Elves' weekly podcast, *No Such Thing as a Fish*, which can be found at qi.com/podcast.

JAMES & THE TWO JOHNS

Index

This is here to help you find your favourite bits.
Like the facts themselves, we've kept it as simple as we can.

B7 chord 259; babies 92, 93, 122, 174, 175, 233, 278, 287, 308, 309, 352; baby walkers 172; bachelors 177, 315; backside 176; bacteria 71, 213, 252, 349; badgers 282; badminton 69; Lake Baikal 43; bakers 177; balancing 249; Christian Bale 283; balloons 77; Ban Ki-moon 30; bananas 67, 68, 287; bank accounts 135; bank holidays 113; bank raids 247; banknotes 157, 317, 349; bankruptcy 189; banks 189; bans 119, 172, 227, 245, 246, 290, 295, 337, 338; baptism 186, 345; Barbados 298; Barcelona 241; Mercedes Barcha 181; *barf* 111; barking 264; Barney Rubble 304; barrels 16, 186, 191; J. M. Barrie 120, 227; bartenders 189; baseball 95; baseball gloves 239; basketball 37, 170; bathrooms 258; baths 154, 315; *Batman* 283; Batman, Turkey 283; bats (*see also* fruit bats) 117; batteries 30; battle 352; BBC 242; BBC licence fee 242; beaches 70, 241, 324; Beam me up, Scotty 207; beans 127; beards 132, 294, 295; bears 12, 142, 282; beating 92; beauty 301; beavers 5; beds 60, 229, 310, 352; beef 202, 296; Mr Beene 223; beer 204; bees 217; beetles 65, 102, 176, 177, 328; Mrs Beeton 260; beheading 44, 57, 58, 210; Beijing 17, 131, 341; Belarus 287; Belarusians 287; belief 289, 345; bells 101; Gurbanguly Berdimuhamedow 56; bergy seltzer 111; Berlin 121; Jeff Bezos 66; Bible 225, 289, 295, 343; bicycles 66; big C 198; Big Macs 153; bikinis 241; bills 95; Osama bin Laden 262; bingo 94; biofuel 159, 184; biologists 282; bird flu 13; birds 138, 216, 249, 263, 327; Birmingham 287; biros 130; birth rate 64; births 18, 64, 89, 92, 143, 278, 287, 288, 290, 352; bisexuality 235; bitch the pot 285; biting 47, 95, 290, 335; *Bittium* 328; Aloe Blacc 292; black 115, 116, 351; Black Cocks 69; black holes 115, 212; Blackbeard 308; bladders 116; *Blade Runner* 224; blasphemy 172; blenders 218; Clarence Blethen 95; blind people 60; blinking 37, 123;

Cabinet 268; cacti 99, 149; Cadbury's 214, 288; Cadillacs 144; caffeine 196; cakes 77, 269; calendars 114; Robert Calf 291; California 333; California mite 329; Calle Me Falta un Tornillo, Valladolid 350; calories 203, 204, 279; Cambridge University 262; camels 12; Cameron 165; James Cameron 223; camouflage 298; Canada 5, 63, 171, 172; canaries 3, 253; Canary Islands 93; cancer 198; candidates 105, 160; canes 117; Cannes Film Festival 142; cannibalism 58, 278; Canterbury 225; Cape Town 288; capital cities 148; Al Capone 144; Frank Capra 326; captivity 290; car exhaust 285; car parks 285; caribou 111; carp 110; Lewis Carroll 84; carrots 126; cars 6, 8, 13, 24, 78, 81, 109, 144, 184, 258; Casanova 244; cash (*see also* money) 285; Johnny Cash 32; Le Casserole 220; Catholics 137, 345; cats 3, 10, 11, 27, 49, 103, 104, 105, 290; CCTV 33, 34; ceasefires 250; cellophane 76; cells 131, 197; censorship 108; cereal 326; chameleons 96; champagne 16, 17, 41; Charlie Chaplin 25; characters 73, 85, 145, 189, 206, 221, 266, 281, 282, 283, 293, 304, 305, 336; charity 135; Prince Charles 184; Charles VIII 95; Charleston 246; *Charlotte's Web* 311; *charqui* 220; chat shows 56; Geoffrey Chaucer 178, 225, 226; Hugo Chávez 56; cheating 177; cheeks 88, 124; Cheese 278; cheese 27, 28, 64, 93, 278; cheesy 93; cheetahs 24, 264, 329; Anton Chekhov 4; chemicals 132, 153, 213, 287, 328; chess 91, 150, 246, 301; Chessington World of Adventures 290; G. K. Chesterton 227; chests 211; Chewbacca 282; chewing gum 133; Chicago 8, 171; Chichi Jima 58; chicken nuggets 217, 341; chicken salesmen 291; chickens 91, 215, 216, 217, 309, 341; children 3, 21, 64, 78, 79, 88, 120, 121, 124, 139, 143, 146, 178, 180, 186, 195, 215, 243, 270, 336; Chile 322; Chilean 25; chimpanzees 84; China 15, 16, 61, 110, 121, 145, 188, 300, 343; the Chinese 60,

64, 98, 233; Chinese burn 145; Chinese food 341; chips (*see also* French fries) 276; chirping 327; chisels 272; chlorine 213; chocolate 50, 211, 214, 234; chocolate creams 269; chocolate-chip cookies 234; 'Chopsticks' 299; chopsticks 299; Christianity 114, 340; Christmas 30, 273; chromosome 1 328; *chummery* 177; Winston Churchill 16, 29, 193; cider 118, 186; cigarettes 141, 153; cinemas 35; circumcision 199; circuses 66, 161; cities 248, 249; clams 197; classical music 52; Nick Clegg 149; Cleopatra 87, 143, 339; Cleopatra's Needle 143; clicking 117, 319; climbing 102, 234; Clinton, Montana 166; clothing 79, 135, 153, 298, 301; clotted cream 12; clouds 230, 333; clover 274; clowns 171; Club 18–30 181; clubs 268; coastal waters 70; coastline 70; coat hanger 310; cocaine 105, 297, 305; cockney 178; cockroaches 56, 175, 176; coconuts 145; cod 300; coffee 196, 262, 286; coffee beans 263; coincidence 251; coins 48, 85, 156, 157, 190, 349; Coldplay 32; Phil Collins 89; Colonel Sanders 292; colours 238, 239; *Columbia* space shuttle 37; Christopher Columbus 163; combinations and permutations 41, 320; comedians 318, 337; comfort zone 94; comic strips 304; comical 178; commercials 32; commonplaceness 34, 138, 164, 182, 187, 222, 279, 303, 304, 347, 349; communism 321; community service 149; company chairmen 322; complaints 69; complexions 173; computers 153, 161, 222, 262; Arthur Conan Doyle 227; concrete 6; conductors (heat) 169; confusion 290; conkers 142; Joseph Conrad 311; Conservative Party 165; conspiracy 318; John Constable 295; consummation 209; container ships 67, 103; contamination 348; contempt of court 147; contraceptives 244; *conversesjukan* 241; convicts 323; Cook Islands 260; Cookie Monster 282; cooking 126, 260, 277; cooling 99; co-operation 169; Copenhagen (horse) 269;

depression 38, 290; depth 332, 333; Derbisol 21; René
Descartes 38; deserts 136; design 76, 171, 319; desks 191,
226; Detroit 102; Frankie Dettori 173; devil 199, 276, 345;
de-worming 105; diagnoses 290; diamonds 114, 117; diaries
151; Philip K. Dick 224; Charles Dickens 3, 171; Francis
Dickens 171; dictionaries 202; digestive system 11, 237;
digging up 58; dildos 2; dimples 88; dinner 177; Celine Dion
201; diplodocuses 267; disarmament 47; disinfecting 212;
disner 177; Disney 281, 282; distance 6, 38, 111, 136, 156;
distraction 162; divine protection 302; diving 332; diving
board 148; division 76; divorce 61, 89, 179, 191; Dmitri, son
of Ivan the Terrible 101; *Dr Jekyll and Mr Hyde* 310; *Doctor
Who* 170; dogcollarane 328; dogs 3, 12, 105, 118, 122, 123,
130, 134, 194, 249, 273, 282; d'oh 221; dollars 157; Domesday
Book 225; domestication 269; Doncaster 315; doorknobs
212; doormen 322; Doris 159; Doritos 277; dormice 240;
Dorset 291; doughnuts 176; drag artists 337; drains 251;
Sir Francis Drake 255; dream team 94; dreams 60, 61, 310;
dresses 301, 310; drinking 16, 52, 95, 110, 118, 149, 196,
229, 286, 287; drive-through 341; driving 6, 81, 201; driving
test 223; drones 59; droppings 13, 270; drugs 101, 215, 306;
druids 193; drunkenness 209; dry cleaning 153; Dubai 24;
Dublin 91; ducks 163, 296; dung 53, 156, 205; Dungeness
Nature Reserve 136; Dunkin' Donuts 194; dust 135, 231;
Dutch Crown jewels 238; dwarfs 284; dye 41, 250, 295

ear trumpets 284; ears 177, 312, 334; Earth 70, 71, 72, 131,
141, 230, 256, 281, 302, 332, 333, 342; earthquakes 98, 343;
earthworms 252; eating 52, 58, 67, 68, 75, 80, 104, 121, 122,
124, 125, 159, 173, 177, 196, 202, 212, 214, 254, 260, 267,
269, 275, 276, 279, 288, 296; echidnas 167; echolocation 117;

galaxies 131; Galileo Galilei 18; Francis Galton 315; gambling 7, 301; *Game of Thrones* 232; 'Gangnam Style' 338; gangs 247, 285; gardens 7, 17; James Garfield 144; *gargalesis* 240; gargling 220; garlands 156; *gasfiter* 25; Bill Gates 317; Gaul 204; *gavisti* 25; Haile Gebrselassie 151; *Gelae* 328; gender 13, 14, 15, 23; General Elections 105; genes 133; genetic disorders 198; genetic mutations 214; genomes 248, 309; geological changes 70, 71, 72; St George 239; George IV 209; George Cross 14; Georgian (language) 261; Georgians (period) 260; German forces 250; German language 77, 192, 261, 272, 353; Germans 36, 64, 78, 107; Germany 39, 108, 142, 271; germs 103; Ghana 20, 110; *Gift* 272; gift cards 272; gifts 4, 10, 135; Gila monster 306; gingerbread men 310; girls 92, 232, 299, 308, 345; Giza 297; Glasgow 137; glass 130; Gloucestershire 136; glue 124; goats 97, 140, 296; God 35, 225, 303; 'God Save the Queen' 68; Godloves Solicitors 292; gods 149, 159; Joseph Goebbels 170; Wolfgang von Goethe 304; gold 48, 131, 164, 333; Museum of Gold 88; Whoopi Goldberg 89; goldfish 61, 279; gold rush 333; golf 200, 201, 353; golf ball liver 201; golf balls 66, 200, 201; golf carts 201; golf courses 201; *Gone with the Wind* 338; Good Friday 39; Google 140, 151, 152; googolplex 152; Victor Goulet 324; GPS 319; grades 14, 304; Grand Canyon 19; Grand National 303; Grandma Moses 237; grandparents 209; grapes 118, 230; grapples 118; grass 39, 140, 235; grasshoppers 235; graves 277, 349; *Gravity* 224; Great Britain 9, 21, 30, 33, 42, 54, 107, 112, 136, 154, 184, 191, 197, 223, 259, 272, 288, 322, 323, 327, 348, 349, 352; Great Depression (US) 157; Great Famine (1845) 121; Great Wall of China 121, 256; Greece 25, 179, 216; Greek 1, 72, 119, 216; Greeks 50, 53, 88, 159, 315; *Green Eggs and Ham* 288; Greenery Day 113; Pope Gregory I 159; grey 238;

International Trade Union Confederation 321; International
Years 307; Internet 29, 34, 135, 186, 325; Inuit language 261;
Inuits 100; invasion 63, 271; inventions 43, 76, 81, 107, 151,
153, 219, 277, 291, 309; inventors 7, 23, 65, 151, 223, 229, 234,
277, 297, 310; 'Invictus' 73; iPad 11; Iran 107, 119, 146, 337;
Iraq 1, 10, 257; Ireland 74, 91, 121, 202, 350; irons 250; Islam
114; islands 70; Italian accent 183; Italians 183, 184, 322;
Italy 222; *It's a Wonderful Life* 326; *Ittibittium* 328; Ivan the
Terrible 101; Vyacheslav Ivanov 164; *izikhothane* 285

Michael Jackson 170; Jade 299; jaguars 130; jam 194; Jamaica
112; *James and the Giant Peach* 51; Jameson's Irish whiskey
229; Japan 113, 149, 182, 246, 249, 320, 339; the Japanese 60,
149, 181, 182, 251, 353; Japanese companies 155; Japanese
language 261; jars 98, 210; javelins 43; Jehovah's Witnesses
302; jelly 124; jellyfish 37, 132, 219; Jenny, ship's cat 103;
jerky 220; Jerome K. Jerome 227; Jesus 138; jet lag 8;
jewellery 243; Jews 306; Jiangsu 15; Jimmy (raven) 326; jobs
31, 55, 89, 164, 194, 222, 278, 292; John 63; John O'Groats
132; Empress Josephine 46; journalists 26, 56; judges 147;
juice 218; Julius Caesar 33; jumbo jets 270; junk 152; Just Do
It 266; Just Missed It Club 103

Franz Kafka 311; Kansas City 217; *kaput* 58; John F. Kennedy
55, 56, 86; Kent 33, 136; Clark Kent 283; kerosene 153; Jack
Kerouac 156; keys 271; *khaki* 231; Khaleesi 232; Khasi Hills
231; kidneys 215; killing 134; kilts 302; Kim Il-sung 338;
Kim Jong-un 338; kimonos 68, 320; kinglets 173; kings 173;
Rudyard Kipling 227; kissing 40, 245, 273, 274, 290; Jason
Kitcat 233; kitchen chair 94; kitchen sink 103; KitKat 233;
kiwi fruit 253; kiwis 288; Calvin Klein 130; knees 217;

Marianas Trench 332; *Marie Celeste* 16; marijuana 106; marine animals 159; marmalade 218; Gabriel García Márquez 181; marriage 173, 191, 209; Mars 90, 124, 281; marshes 257; George R. R. Martin 232; Martini 110; Maryland 147; Mass 146; Masters in Lunacy 68; maternity leave 78; mating (*see also* sex) 9, 45, 98, 236, 347; maturing 186; Mauritania 188; Mayan culture 114; mayors 129, 283; mazes 271; MDR 162; meals 52, 126, 237; meanings 1, 25, 93, 94, 100, 140, 142, 160, 162, 165, 177, 178, 205, 260, 261, 289; meat 149, 296, 340; meatballs 53; medals 26, 138, 153, 163, 164; medical bills 189; medical conditions 199; medical mistakes 316; medication 32, 105; medicine 54, 297; meh 339; melonettes 253; melting 112; mementoes (*see also* souvenirs) 56; memory 206, 289; men 13, 15, 55, 65, 71, 75, 78, 83, 96, 98, 119, 132, 134, 180, 191, 279, 301, 350; Dmitri Mendeleev 278; mental health 322; mercury 244; meringue 203; metal 169, 214; meteoroids 342; Mexicans 158; Mexico 63; miaow 49; mice 13, 80, 104, 228, 240, 243; Michigan 147; Micronesia 260; Middle Ages 178, 204; Middle East 136; milk 12, 54, 77, 93, 167, 168, 174, 219, 278; milk teeth 243; milk thistle 327; Milky Way 92; millionaires 222; millipedes 53; A. A. Milne 227; Min 49; mind 79; 'Mind Your Business' 157; mine clearance 10; mineral water 147, 242; Mini 76; miniskirts 241; mint tea 250; Miramax 35; mirrors 23; missing items, *see* lost things; missionaries 149, 302; Mississippi 188; Missouri 189; misspell 138; mites 329; mobile homes 33; mobile phones 147, 161, 348; Mogadishu 9; molecules 328; molluscs 98; *Mona Lisa* 258; monarchs 44, 143, 258; Mondays 247; money (*see also* cash) 34, 148, 157, 254, 255, 256, 260, 317; Chris Moneymaker 293; Mongolia 269; mongooses 4; monkeys 10; Monopoly 114, 255; Montana 166; Montenegrin 110;

Nigeria 26, 35, 190, 242; Nigerian electric power authority (NEPA) 242; night 21, 81; night vision 344; nightclubs 159; nightmares 60; Nike 266; nipples 167; nitrogen 237, 305; Alfred Nobel 277; Nobel Prizes 54, 191, 232; noon 90; Morton Norbury 294; Normandy 214; North Korea 26, 338; Northern Hemisphere 99; Northern Ireland 91, 137; Northern Territory, Australia 300; Northwest Territories, Canada 63; Norway 70, 146, 158, 172, 258; Norwegian language 241; Norwegians 211; noses 13, 249; notebooks 90; nouns 347; novelists 191, 227, 311; Now, now! 94; nuclear safety 189; nuclear weapons 223, 342; nudism 234, 262; numbers 139; nurses 353

oak trees 179; Oasis 32; Barack Obama 300; obesity 195; Obsession for Men 130; oceans (*see also* sea) 44, 213, 331, 332; octopuses 46, 47, 247, 318; King Offa 143; Offa's Dyke 143; office hours 76; office workers 125; offices 14, 88; Olav V of Norway 258; old maids 128; oligodynamic effect 212; olive oil 315; Olympic Games 25, 26, 27, 131, 132, 153, 163, 163, 243, 323, 341; omelettes 91; *On the Road* 156; Onan 253; onesies 290; onions 275; online activity 325; *onychophagia* 198; 'Oops! ... I Did It Again' 57; opinion polls 33; opium 105, 277, 324; optimism 334; orange 115; oranges 64, 331; orang-utans 46; orchids 8; orgasms 347; orgle 220; Oscars 35, 40, 326; Lee Harvey Oswald 87; *otacousticon* 284; *oui* 139; Ouija boards 154; ovaries 237, 263; ovens 78; overdose 316; ovulation 264; Oxford University 18, 299; Oyster card 255; oysters 211; ozone layer 200

Pacific Ocean 136, 331; pain 86; paint 213, 296, 326; paintings 295, 296; Pakistan 87; Pakistanis 88; Palermo 97; palm trees

Saab 227; *saboka* 282; sacrifices 211; Sahara desert 135, 188;
St Lucia 180; salad 276, 289; salamanders 37, 46, 85, 251,
307; sales 67, 129, 226, 295, 303, 305, 348; J. D. Salinger 3;
saliva 306; salmon 130, 219; salt 44, 174; saluting 350;
salvation 302; Samoa 166; San Francisco 34; sand 188, 214,
331; sandals 319; Earl of Sandwich 74; sandwiches 74, 106,
124, 125; Sanskrit 25; 'Santa Claus Is Coming to Town' 30;
Sasmuan, Philippines 40; Satan 303; Saudi Arabia 55, 57,
119, 192, 193; sauerkraut 121; sausages 107, 112; saving lives
316; scales (fish) 116; scars 259; scatomancy 100; Harrison
Schmitt 125; school (education) 14, 149, 151, 251, 322; school
fees 323; schools (fish) 116; Arnold Schwarzenegger 224;
science fiction 223; scientists 70, 262; Scotland 9, 137, 186,
300, 302; Scotsmen 302; Ridley Scott 224; Scottish Official
Board of Highland Dancing 302; Scrabble 139, 228; scurvy
179; sea (*see also* oceans) 66, 333; sea level 333; sea otters 47;
sea snails 328; sea squirts 46; seahorses 92; seamstresses 301;
seasoning 48; seasons 38; seatbelts 154; seats 202; seaweed
90; Second World War 3, 29, 83, 108, 142, 155; secrecy 108,
318, 351; secretaries 307; secretions 124; seeds 253, 263; self
help 303; selling 67, 147; semen 49, 50, 245; Serengeti 264;
seriousness 64; Dr Seuss 49, 288; sewage 158; sewers 164;
sewing 301, 315; sex (*see also* mating) 9, 10, 23, 45, 61, 98,
175, 203, 220, 236, 290, 307, 346; Sexmoan, Philippines 40;
sexpert 94; sexting 220; sexual lubricants 306; sexually
transmitted diseases 8, 28; SHAFTAs 34; Shandong 15;
shape 125, 176; shares 50; *The Shark and the Sardines* 87;
sharks 45; shaving 182; sheep 81, 291, 339, 340; sheet music
67; shellfish 47, 211; shells 247, 344; *shemomedjamo* 260; Alan
Shepard 124; Sherlock 233; *Sherlock* 233; Shetland Islands
34; shins 246; Shintoism 149; ships 66, 67, 103, 179, 213, 302;

shipwrecks 180; shoes 128, 129, 319, 320; shooting 55, 267; shoplifting 27; shops 9, 55, 74; shortages 102; showers 275; shrimps 211; shrines 97; shrouds 87; Siberia 101; Sichuan 15; Sicily 97; sick leave 247; sickness 53; sighted people 60; sign language 23; signs 9, 23, 76, 350; *The Silence of the Lambs* 266; silent films 318; silicone 351; silk 41, 169; silkworms 41; silver 29, 271, 301; *Silybum* 327; Homer Simpson 189, 221; *The Simpsons* 221; Frank Sinatra 275; Singapore 147; singing 21, 30, 257; singlewoman 128; sinking 103, 331; sisters 208, 209; size 37, 45, 54, 62, 67, 70, 71, 90, 91, 112, 113, 121, 128, 129, 136, 140, 150, 152, 166, 200, 217, 228, 235, 237, 239, 264, 281, 288, 309, 328, 341, 347; skateboards 172; skeletons 97, 112; Skips 300; skyscrapers 15; slang 94, 128, 168, 202, 285, 327; slavery 18; sleeping 20, 21, 59, 60, 61, 229, 308, 309, 310; sliced bread 19; slime mould 328; slogans 137, 157, 266; sloth 102; Slovakians 185; Slovenians 139, 185; slums 212; smelling 60; smells 13, 27, 39, 130, 133, 241, 335; smiley face 266; smoke 53; smoking 105, 141, 199, 352; smuggling 125; smurfs 350; snails 213, 308, 328; snake charming 2; snakes 2, 3, 53, 211, 252, 312, 335; sneezing 10; sniffer dogs 249; snow 111, 326; snow goggles 111; Snowflame 305; soap 316; sociability 235; socks 144, 319; Socrates 52; soft drinks 196; soil 17; soldiers 88, 105, 250; Somali language 160; Somalia 9, 78; Somalis 57; songs 56, 57, 73; sonic boom 80; sorry 182; souls 175; *The Sound of Music* 74; sounds 22, 111, 117; soup 218; South Africa 235, 285; South America 330; South Pole 111; Southend-on-Sea 171; Southern Hemisphere 99; souvenirs (*see also* mementoes) 272; soy sauce 48; space 125, 207, 346; space travel 44, 280; spacecraft 44; spacesuits 346; Spain 148, 172, 350; Spaniards 294, 350; Spanish language 77, 148, 183; Spanish navy 180; sparrowsfart 327; Sparta 173;

Table Mountain 288; table tennis 161; tablets 195; tadpoles
306; *tåfis* 241; Taiwan 26; takeaways 340; Taliban 227;
talking 111, 205; tan lines 312; tanks 80; tapping 117;
tardigrades 331; taste 174, 185, 214; taste buds 176; tattoo
pen 223; tattoos 96; tea 250, 285; teaching 222, 259;
tears 35, 44; teeth (*see also* false teeth) 116, 164, 195, 243;
television 38, 56, 126, 206, 207; television sets 153; telling the
future 100; temperature 50, 99, 100, 117, 169, 334; Shirley
Temple 20; tempura 149; tennis 95; tequila 117; *Terminator
2* 224; termites 130; terrorists 57; Terry's 50; Tesco 276;
Nikola Tesla 121; testicles 98, 166, 237, 252, 264; Testy
Fest 166; Texas 2, 101; *The Texas Chainsaw Massacre* 266;
textile industry 135; *textopornographique* 220; Thailand 26;
Thanksgiving 113; theft 27, 29, 79, 291, 350; thermostats 88;
thighs 97; *This Is the End* 225; Thomas 63; thoughts 152;
threesomes 45; throats 86; throwing 10, 50, 55, 153; throwing
away 126, 215; tickling 141, 240; tie-breakers 160; ties 320;
tigers 1; Tightwad, Missouri 189; time capsules 271; *Time*
Person of the Year 347; time travel 115; *The Times* 47, 83,
246; tipping the hat 350; tissues 155; *Titanic* (film) 223;
Titanic (liner) 103; titles 36, 51, 238; toads 343, 344; toddlers
195; toes 129, 241; Toilet Duck 76; toilet paper 102; toilets
(*see also* lavatories) 75, 102, 103, 155, 172; J. R. R. Tolkien
69, 232; Michael Tolkien 69; tombstones 352; Tonga 260;
tongues 37; tongue-twisters 36; tooth decay 243; tooth fairy
243; toothpaste 12, 243; tortoises 344; Tory 165; toshers
164; touching 344; tourism 256; tourists 272; town signs 9;
toxicity (*see also* poisons) 12, 13, 118; *Toy Story* 293; toys 106;
trade regulations 287; traffic lights 81; traffic offences 222;
traffic wardens 171; train journeys 314; train stations 155;
trainers 241; trains 79; trampling 321; trampoline 148;

verbs 23; vertigo 37; Viagra 208; vibrations 343; Queen
Victoria 68, 243, 295; Victorians 64, 68, 168, 171; Vietnam
War 105; Vikings 204, 352; Village People 32; violins 23;
Virginia 146, 296; virgins 92, 181; virility 208; virtual reality
145; viruses 141; vision 80; visor 350; vitamin C 142; vocal
sacs 306; voicemail 186; voices 282, 353; Voldemort 336;
volume 48, 67, 77, 158; Volvo 154; Maria von Trapp 74; Kurt
Vonnegut 227; vote rigging 145; voters 105; vultures 97, 245

wagons 100; waiters 324; Ruth Wakefield 234; waking 21,
59; Wales 274; walking 84, 85, 158, 313; wallabies 324;
wallpaper 210; walruses 97, 282; waltz 246; *wamblecropt*
215; war 3, 14, 25, 59, 96, 105, 142, 250; War of the Triple
Alliance 96; Warner Bros 282; warriors 134; washing 155,
161, 199, 205, 316; George Washington 149; Washington
DC 183; waste 30, 185; water 43, 53, 100, 109, 147, 205, 213,
231, 242, 270, 281, 286, 331, 332, 333, 334; water beds 223;
water slides 217; watercolours 296; Waterloo Bridge 245;
wax 307; John Wayne 198; Ron Wayne 50; wealth 222,
248, 254; weather 230; weather forecast 206; webcams 262;
websites 325; wedding night 209, 211; weeds 8; weeper 351;
weight 48, 124, 173, 174, 211, 254, 260, 263, 273, 279, 313;
Harvey Weinstein 35; Duke of Wellington 74, 268, 269; H. G.
Wells 227; Welsh 163; the West 345; Archibald Clark West
277; Westminster Abbey 255; wetness 231; whales 12, 45,
174, 312; whatever 242; wheat 309; *wheeple* 285; whisky 186,
229, 286; whistles 122; whistling 285; white 81, 87, 250, 326;
E. B. White 311; white lead 259; widows 191; Wild West 94;
William 63; wills 255, 297; Harold Wilson 149; Wimbledon
161; wind 230; wine 16, 27, 52, 184, 185, 230; wine glasses
52; wings 92; winnings 293; Kate Winslet 65; winter 38, 90,

121; wire 310; witchcraft 193; wives 89, 96, 104, 210, 222; wizards 69; P. G. Wodehouse 227; Wojtek 142; wolves 211, 250; wombs 228; women 13, 14, 15, 38, 50, 55, 71, 75, 78, 92, 93, 128, 180, 181, 192, 193, 244, 245, 287, 290, 299, 301, 310, 320, 346; Wonga 349; wood-chopping 172; wooden legs 26; woodlice 236; woodpeckers 211; Woody 293; wool 340; Wool, Dorset 291; woolly mammoths 19; words 25, 34, 36, 49, 58, 80, 83, 84, 94, 100, 110, 138, 139, 140, 160, 162, 163, 177, 178, 205, 207, 215, 216, 220, 221, 224, 230, 238, 241, 260, 261, 265, 266, 288, 313; work (*see also* jobs) 28, 54, 55, 152, 159, 190; work places 152, 340; work rates 54; world 5, 15, 16, 18, 25, 33, 35, 36, 39, 41, 62, 67, 91, 93, 98, 99, 103, 106, 112, 114, 130, 144, 145, 150, 180, 181, 209, 213, 214, 217, 222, 231, 234, 239, 248, 252, 254, 262, 264, 301, 303, 310, 313, 318, 333, 338, 339, 340, 348; world champions 161, 293; world records 47, 194, 217; worms 176, 252; worship 149; *World of Warcraft* 145; writing 83

X 126; X-ray slap 342

Yahoo 140, 292; yawning 123, 240; Yazidis 257; yellow 115, 181, 287; yes 139; 'Yes, We Have No Bananas' 67; Yoda 293; yoga mats 153; yoghurt 71; *You Only Live Once* 334; John Young 125; young people 246; Tom Youngs 173; Susilo Bambang Yudhoyono 56

Zeppelins 77; Zimbabwe 256; Zimbabweans 256; Zimbabwe Banking Corporation 256; zip wires 148; zombies 193; zoos 4, 269; Zulu 163; zzz 228